This manual is dedicated to my grandmother, Mildred Ellen Orton, who continues to teach me that kindness and open mindedness can change the world more than any book.

—Cabot Orton

Lights, Camera, Community Video:
Engaging Citizens in Creating a Community Documentary and Vision

CABOT ORTON, KEITH SPIEGEL, AND EDDIE GALE

TABLE OF CONTENTS

Acknowledgments vii

Preface ix

Editor's Note xi

DVD Instructions xii

Part 1. Why a Community Video Project? 1
    What Is a Community Video Project? 2
    The Purpose of This Report 3
    Using Your Community Resources 4
    Preparing Your Community for a Video 5
    Mobilizing Your Steering Committee 7
    Creating the Right Video 9
    How Much Will the Video Cost and
        How Will We Pay for It? 10

Part 2. Pre-production: Equipment and Scheduling 17
    Equipment You'll Need 17
    Selecting an Interview Location 24
    Assembling the Production Crew 24
    Historical Research 26
    Publicity: Getting the Word Out 28
    Scheduling the Shoot 29

Part 3. You're Ready to Go! 33
    Documentary Release Form 33
    Basics of the Video Shoot 34
    The Art of the Interview 40
    Shooting the Video 41

Part 4. Post-production: After the Shoot 45
    Writing the Editing Script 46
    Arranging Editing Facilities 52
    Editing Your Community Video 53

Part 5. Premiering Your Video: Taking the Show on the Road 57
    The Grand Premiere 57
    The Screening 60
    The Feedback Session 61
    Other Uses for Your Video 62
    Evaluating Your Video 65

Appendices 69
    Glossary 69
    Useful Resources 73

ACKNOWLEDGMENTS

The authors would like to thank the following people and organizations without whose help the production of this manual would not of been possible: Bennett Boeschenstein; Dace Carver; Dan Flenniken; Bob Hopkins; Ron Kilburn; Paul Markowitz; Matt McCarthy; Hayes McCarthy; Greg Mikolai; Roger Perry; Vi Sis; Jenna Speer; Fran Stoddard; Ken Sweetzer; Abby Sweetzer; Helen Whyte; Champlain College, Burlington, Vermont; KRMJ Public Television in Grand Junction, Colorado; the Vermont Community Foundation; the Village and Town of Swanton, Vermont; the City of Fruita, Colorado; Morristown, Vermont; Brandon, Vermont; and Brattleboro, Vermont.

The Orton Family Foundation developed the Community Video Project as part of its mission to help citizens of rural and small town America define the future, shape the growth, and preserve the heritage of their communities. This manual and other Orton Family Foundation programs are designed to (1) develop and deliver innovative community land-use planning tools and processes; (2) promote citizen participation in community decision making; and (3) provide education, training, and information resources to citizens, community leaders, and professional planners to more effectively manage growth.

For more information on The Orton Family Foundation, visit the web site at **www.orton.org.**

PREFACE

Even if you're picking up this manual for the first time, you probably already know this: more people than ever before are using the exceptional power of visual media to get what they want. Advertisers know this. Politicians know this. Religious leaders know this. In order to get what they want, these people need something first: *your attention*.

The Orton Family Foundation developed Community Video Projects because these projects promised to be a tremendously effective means of getting people's attention. A visual representation of your community can lead the people within it to convene, to reflect, to visualize, and to act on some of the community's most important issues for the future. This manual was designed to help you, the producer of your community's documentary vision of itself, to interact powerfully with your community, using technology that most people own and anyone can get.

Community Video is about getting people *involved*, which is difficult to do in a world where work and entertainment consume so much of our attention, and professional attention-getters consume much of the rest. The biggest challenge you'll face isn't money, or equipment problems, or time. It's apathy. The fact that you're reading this manual means you are willing to face that challenge. Believe us, it's worth facing.

This manual places a very strong emphasis on being resourceful and on reaching out. We've distilled the most pertinent information and ideas from our own Community Video Projects, to be combined with additional reference sources and inserts. In an appendix to this document is a long list of references covering just about every topic you'll need to produce your own video, regardless of prior experience. Information, along with inspiration, will be your most valuable tool.

Now go out and make a difference in your community.

Cabot Orton
Keith Spiegel

EDITOR'S NOTE

This PAS Report is not only historic because it is the 500th report in the series, but because it is also the first report to include a new medium to help achieve its purpose. There is a Digital Video Disc (DVD) included with this report that will illustrate better than any series of pictures or sentences the achievement possible through a Community Video Project. The community videos prepared for Swanton, Vermont, and Fruita, Colorado, by staff from the Orton Family Foundation with the assistance of citizens from those communities are contained on the DVD. Ideally, you will be able to read the report, view the DVD, review the report, and see how you can make a video comparable to the excellent examples from these communities.

A word of explanation may be in order about why we opted to put these videos on DVD. When the Orton Family Foundation contacted the Northern New England Chapter of the American Planning Association about securing a chapter grant to help produce this report, the original idea was to include a VHS tape or a CD-ROM. Research, however, indicated that the VHS tape would be the least desirable format for displaying the quality of these community videos. CD-ROM was technically inadequate to deal with the length of two videos and would compromise the quality of what you could see on your screen. DVD sales, as indicated in the industry literature, are skyrocketing. The quality and cost of producing a DVD also led us in that direction. We hope that all of the readers of this report have access to a DVD player (either a home "box" or a computer with a DVD drive—we had the DVD prepared so that it will play on either type of hardware). We also hope at some point to mount these videos on both the APA web site and the Orton web site. Our ability to do that may be a year or two away as yet.

The instructions for making the DVD work follow. Should you have difficulty in making the DVD work properly, please first consult the APA website (www.planning.org) or the Orton website (www.orton.org) for some troubleshooting assistance. Should you still not be able to operate the DVD, please e-mail PAS Reports (pasreports@planning.org) with your specific problem.

APA, PAS, The Orton Family Foundation, and APA's Northern New England chapter hope that you find this PAS Report a valuable addition to your information on citizen participation and planning. This report marks a new era for PAS Reports, and, as always, we would be happy to hear from you about this report and the DVD or, for that matter, any particular PAS Report or the report series.

Jim Hecimovich
Chief Editor, PAS Reports
April 2001

DVD INSTRUCTIONS:

To access the full text of the PAS Report using the Hybrid-DVD feature:

1) Insert DVD into DVD–ROM drive.

2) Double Click on the DVD icon.

3) You will find a file name "PAS_Report_500-501.pdf."

4) Double Click to view. (Requirements: Windows PC or Macintosh, DVD-ROM drive, and Adobe Acrobat.)

To view the two community videos on the DVD:

1) Open the DVD player on your PC or Mac. (This player will open automatically on some computers.)

2) A menu containing each of the videos will appear on the screen.

3) Select which video you would like to view and double click. Alternately the two community videos can be viewed on your set-top DVD player (i.e., a stand alone player, connected to a television). After loading the DVD into the set-top player, a menu will appear on the television, prompting you to choose between the two videos.

PART 1

Why a Community Video Project?

Citizens in towns across America have long struggled to find ways to discover and articulate a common vision for their community. Our high-speed, hyper-individualized, Internet- and TV-addicted culture currently complicates this struggle, making it difficult to invigorate the community spirit that has always been at the core of the American town. The physical places we live in play less of a role than ever before in our highly mobile, information-fueled lives. It's no longer uncommon to find that residents of suburban and even rural neighborhoods across the country no longer know their next-door neighbors. At the same time, the *sense of place* that has long been the hallmark of rural and small-town America is increasingly diminished. Locally owned, family-operated diners, barber shops, and hardware stores across the nation have been largely replaced by global franchises, such as McDonald's, Supercuts, and Wal-Mart . . . you get the idea. The bottom line is that civic apathy is a very real factor in any discussion of community planning and citizen participation.

Facing such obstacles, how can a town or neighborhood begin to foster a stronger sense of community identity among its citizens? How can a town planning commission determine what its many groups of citizens would like to see happen in their community in the future? How can busy or apathetic residents be motivated to speak publicly about their ideas and participate in the process of creating a future vision for their communities?

A Community Video Project is a very effective way to stimulate community dialogue and inspire citizen participation in community issues. Think of other tools that are used: a written survey, a planning commission session, or a town meeting. A Community Video Project coaxes citizens to come out of the woodwork and reflect about the past, present, and future of their communities. Most importantly, they are drawn to become involved in a way they never have been before.

PART 1 HIGHLIGHTS:

Why a community video project? Because . . .

• a Community Video Project uses the power and excitement of video production to lure residents into convening publicly to discuss the issues and opportunities facing their communities and to consider choices regarding their future.

• citizen participation, communication, and visualization are the essential goals of a Community Video Project, meaning that the process of creating the video will almost certainly end up being more important and valuable than the video itself.

• a Community Video Project can incorporate a wide variety of perspectives, create a widespread sense of local "buy-in," and energize community members in a way that leads to greater communication and networking.

• a video can be produced with a modest budget of $15,000 or even a dirt cheap budget of $2,500, while the returns on that investment can be immeasurable and long lasting.

• you can involve the young people in the community—schools are a great place to look for volunteers, equipment, and expertise.

Two of the authors meet with town citizens to discuss the importance of their Community Video Project. The citizens are ultimately the stars of any such project.

The Community Video Project was founded on three basic premises:

1. The involvement and energy of all citizens is invaluable.
2. Video is an effective tool to capture and synthesize this energy.
3. Positive social change comes about when citizens are recognized and honored for their effort and involvement.

WHAT IS A COMMUNITY VIDEO PROJECT?

A Community Video Project uses the power and excitement of video production to lure residents into convening publicly to discuss the issues and opportunities facing their community, and to consider choices regarding their future. Over the course of 5 to 10 days, or even several weeks, as many citizens as possible are interviewed on camera and encouraged to talk about the past, present, and future of their community. This footage is then reviewed, culled into a script, and edited into a half-hour (or longer) documentary that accurately reflects what historical events shaped the character of a community, what issues and opportunities it currently faces, and what its future may look like.

The ultimate goal of a Community Video Project, however, is not simply to create a documentary or to develop a promotional video about the merits of a town. Because citizen participation, communication, and visualization are the essential goals of a Community Video Project, *its process is inherently more important than the final product*. The citizens you want to reach become the co-producers, the production assistants, the caterers, and, most importantly, the stars of the project. They want to be involved. And they can't be involved in this project without thinking deeply about their community.

This manual is based on the experiences of The Orton Family Foundation in producing Community Video Projects in five rural communities in Vermont and Colorado. In the process of creating these half-hour documentaries, we simultaneously documented the procedures involved in creating the videos and using the production process to engage the community. Our hope is that communities across the country can use this report as a field guide to successfully undertake video projects on their own.

The five towns in which The Orton Family Foundation has produced Community Video Projects range in population from 4,000 to 10,000 residents. Some of the major issues highlighted in the videos include:

- fast-food chains and mini-malls taking over the outskirts of town;
- a new Wal-Mart in a neighboring community;
- the economic viability of a fragile historic district with numerous buildings on the National Historic Register;
- heavy truck traffic passing through a historic downtown business district and the implications of a truck bypass;
- the destruction of the downtown historic district by fire;
- the closing of a major local employer;
- a transition to a bedroom community;
- a volatile mix of "old timers and newcomers";
- the legacy of a boom/bust economy based on natural resources;
- a jurisdiction's role as an industrial, commercial, and government services hub for the county;
- excellent public schools, outdoor recreation, and quality-of-life opportunities;
- conserving community spirit;
- a rivalry with neighboring towns; and
- an aging nuclear power plant.

THE PURPOSE OF THIS MANUAL

This report is designed to aid *you*, the producer. To do that, we are going to make some assumptions about who you are.

We assume you have an interest both in video production and in the well-being of your community and other communities like yours. You might be a local, regional, or neighborhood planner who wants to work

The five towns in which The Orton Family Foundation has produced Community Video Projects range in population from 4,000 to 10,000 residents.

Creating a video involves collaboration, resourcefulness, and diligent research.

with a local tech center, college, or public access channel to produce this video. You could be a volunteer on a planning commission, head of your local historical society, or an instructor at your high school's new video lab. You are definitely someone willing to put together a team to produce your Community Video.

This manual will be your unofficial Production Field Guide, to be used before, during, and after the undertaking of a Community Video Project. We created this report based on some elementary values.

USING YOUR COMMUNITY RESOURCES
Maximizing Collaboration and Teamwork Within a Community

You can't produce a Community Video on your own. The extraordinary wealth of information you will need, as well as most of the resources, reside within the community. Since you ultimately want your community to "own" the video, make your fellow community members your partners. Rely on them to identify key local issues and topics to be covered by a video project and contact other citizens who might give particularly good interviews about specific topics. Ask about the most scenic locations in the community, and you'll be deluged with favorites. Put out the call for important archival and historical information, such as books, photographs, and film footage, and residents will rummage through their closets as well as point you to the local historical society. Once you've developed this level of cooperation on the project within the community, suddenly it doesn't seem as difficult to ask for office space with a phone, to borrow equipment, or access other important resources. Which leads us to . . .

Being Resourceful

A Community Video Project requires its producers to draw upon the resources of their community and then put those resources to use with techniques outlined in this report. Included are equipment resources (such as a camcorder from a public access station or a borrowed motorboat to capture footage on a river), location resources (such as borrowed office space or a free screening venue), and staff resources (volunteers to help with the shoot and in the production office). The result of all this "resource-wrangling" is a video truly created by and reflective of the community in which it was produced. Resourcefulness is also the most important quality of a good producer. It can make up for almost any shortcoming in a video production budget. In short, let adversity become opportunity.

Conducting Diligent Research

Remember that a Community Video Project will be viewed by the most knowledgeable critics you will ever encounter—the community's residents. If there are any glaring inaccuracies about historical information, statistics, occupational titles, or name spellings in the final product, you'll be hearing about it for some time. Your goal is to create a portrait of a community and its character that is as accurate and balanced as possible. The objective is to synthesize the maximum attainable number of viewpoints from citizens, mainstream and otherwise, into a finished piece that is honest, coherent, and, you hope, artful. In order to achieve this complexity and balance in a video project, it's important to keep an ear out for dissenting viewpoints, for quirky tidbits of information, for both obvious and subtle issues that a community presents, and for the often random but revealing qualities about a community that arise from discussions with citizens on the street.

Planning for Long-Term Use

Your video will have a variety of uses, from the catalyst for a community planning session, to an elementary school classroom civics discussion, to use in a legislative committee hearing discussing funding for your truck bypass. You have the enviable task of producing a video that will be suitable for all ages, substantive and entertaining, and able to stand the test of time. Good Luck!

PREPARING YOUR COMMUNITY FOR A VIDEO

The ultimate purpose of a Community Video Project is to inspire citizens to visualize and shape the future of their communities. This process takes place by fulfilling four basic goals: getting citizens to convene, to reflect, to visualize, and, finally, to act.

Local citizens know their community best. Creating their own production, as these citizens did in Swanton, Vermont, brings a sense of empowerment, focus, and energy that is often lacking in other citizen participation planning efforts.

A "convention" of all parts of a community, including members from a diverse array of socioeconomic, cultural, and age groups is, unfortunately, a difficult task in today's world.

To convene: A "convention" of all parts of a community, including members from a diverse array of socioeconomic, cultural, and age groups is, unfortunately, a difficult task in today's world. Before citizens can feel like part of a community, they need to see their neighbors face-to-face and to realize that members of a community always have something in common, no matter how trivial.

A Community Video Project convenes residents in three ways. The first is by getting community members involved in the video production process. The second is surreptitious—residents are interviewed as individuals, and then the magic of video transforms their input into part of a 30-minute community discussion. Finally, people are naturally excited about movies and television projects, especially when the movies are about them. A public screening of the video will convene a wide range of residents who want to see what their friends, neighbors, and relatives have to say.

To reflect: Getting people to think at length about how their community came to be, where it is today, and where it may head in the future is a critical function of Community Video. Interviews take participants step-by-step through an open discussion of the past, present, and future of a community. The point here is to get people to think about how the choices and decisions made by citizens result in concrete actions and long-term results, and how historical events and decisions might mirror those of today. With the finished video, the audience will view historical highlights of the community, along with impressions from a variety of citizens, and they inherently reflect on their own impressions of the community.

To visualize: There's a powerful effect when large numbers of people realize that they share common visions and have proposed common actions and solutions that had previously gone publicly unannounced. Leading people from the past to the future (i.e., from the familiar to the unfamiliar) requires a great deal of energetic thinking. Using the visual medium of video accelerates people's ability to picture how they would like the future to be.

To act: Whether the participants of a Community Video ever take the ultimate step—acting upon common visions for the future—is left in the hands of a community and its citizens. First and foremost, action requires a very strong sense of commitment to a visualization, shared by many people, that is truly worth pursuing. The ability to visualize a desired goal greatly enhances the ability of residents to voice their concerns and desires for the future.

Organizing a Steering Committee

The first concrete step to take in producing a Community Video Project should be to organize a steering committee. This group is comprised of a variety of community leaders and citizens who have the time, energy, and motivation to devote to such a project. The steering committee takes responsibility for initiating the production process and overseeing the details and focus of the video. While it's certainly possible to produce a video with a small independent group, creating a steering committee ensures that a video incorporates a wide variety of perspectives, that it creates a widespread sense of local "buy-in," and that some of the more energetic members of a community will spread word of the project in their respective social circles.

To organize a steering committee, compile a wish list of those individuals, organizations, and institutions you would like to have involved. Start with an individual you think shares your enthusiasm and recruit this person to be a champion of the project. Steering committee candidates may include town government officials, business owners, historical society members, farmers, teachers, or the heads of nonprofit organizations. Shoot for a diverse group of people with different perspectives and different contacts throughout the community.

Now it's time to have one-on-one conversations. Stop in at people's offices, catch them at the local diner, or ring them on the phone. Be a bit of a salesperson at first. Once you get a few people on board, others will follow suit. When you have recruited a sufficient cross section of community leaders to participate, you're ready for your first steering committee meeting.

Explaining the Benefits of Community Video

The first steering committee meeting should introduce to potential members of that committee the concept, purpose, and specific benefits behind producing a Community Video. Start with the basics. The 30-minute video will profile the community and interview a number of residents regarding their attitudes about the present and their thoughts about the future. A large number of people in the community are likely to watch the video and consider these issues themselves. Residents will convene, reflect, and visualize in a way they have never done before. Because they have seen their community in a new light, residents may act to make changes or to more clearly establish means to preserve the things that are dear to them.

Get your fellow committee members to articulate how they think the video could benefit the community. It's not hard to get people excited about making a movie, especially if it's about them. Have a free-flowing discussion, or if you need more structure, ask your committee to brainstorm the benefits inherent in each of the subjects listed below. Have them write their ideas on post-it notes or index cards and combine the notes in appropriate categories. Some suggestions and categories you can provide if people have a hard time articulating their ideas are provided in the sidebar.

Review the information the steering committee has generated and be sure you have covered the important topics, especially the following.

How will the video be used? It's important to remember that the primary audience for the video is the community itself. A finished video should receive a public premiere screening and can even be used as a kick-off for a community strategic planning session or other planning event. Other screenings can take place at local schools, churches, or social clubs. Copies of the video can be made available to the town library, historical society, and chamber of commerce. Ideally, the video can be broadcast on public access cable television or even a local PBS station.

How does the community become involved in the production process? The video production requires the involvement of many members of a community in a wide variety of capacities: as people to be interviewed; in helping with the production; in coming forward to contribute old photos, slides, and film footage of a community; in attending the premiere screening; and in the discussions and ongoing reflection generated by the finished video.

How is the footage not included in the finished documentary to be used? The dozens of hours of unused footage don't get thrown away, but will instead be made available to the public as excellent source material for other documentaries and projects. The footage can also serve as a valuable community archive for future residents.

MOBILIZING YOUR STEERING COMMITTEE

The next item on the agenda for the first steering committee meeting should be to determine who in attendance has an interest in committing to the project, and the time and energy to do it. A good rule of thumb for choosing steering committee members is: the people who show up and wind up staying are the right people. This is an organic process and usually those with real time, energy, and inclination to participate in the project sort of choose themselves for their role.

Once everyone has determined who will stay on the committee, start discussing the responsibilities for each member.

The Chairperson

The chairperson is someone who will be so closely involved in the production that he or she can be considered a Co-Producer. This should be a champion of the project who doesn't have to do all the work, but who does have to make sure that someone carries out all of the work tasks. The chairperson will convene and chair steering committee meetings and be the primary liaison between the steering committee and the production crew. The chairperson should also be a spokesperson for the project.

How a video project can benefit a community . . .

The use of the video:
- Documentation of how things have changed over time
- An opportunity to get the community together to think about the future
- New information and historical facts for younger and newer community members
- Citizens learning new things about where they live and how it got that way
- A chance to listen to young people about their interests and goals
- Promotion of the town for business and economic development
- Morale booster for revitalization of the village, downtown, or community
- Affirmation of individual participant's point of view

The process of making the video:
- Increase level of involvement in community, incorporating people of all ages and perspectives
- Bring young and elderly people together
- Get local schools involved
- Teach new hands-on multimedia skills to participants
- Create a new spirit of volunteerism in town

The out-take footage:
- Create a community "family album"
- Create a video or multimedia promotional tool for the community
- Maintain archival information for the historical society and for posterity

Steering Committee

The steering committee is responsible for the following tasks that can be done as a committee, assigned to subcommittees, or taken on by individuals on the committee.

Determine key issues in the community. Develop a list of the important issues and topics that will profile the community, and rank the items on that list according to importance. Consider the issues that will affect planning over the next 5 to 10 years. Examples could include: Housing Boom, Boom and Bust Economy, Relationship with Neighboring Communities, Fragility of Historic Downtown Commercial District.

Select people to interview. Develop a list of approximately 30 people who will be able to address aspects of the key issues you have identified. Ideally, these will be people from many different walks of life who are articulate and can express their ideas clearly on camera. The list can include people from city government, chamber of commerce members and local business owners, people from volunteer commissions and government agencies, farmers or ranchers, religious community members, and students or other local youth.

Identify historical photos and documents. List the important historical events that have shaped the community. Locate historic photos, maps, and other documents to illustrate historic local events. Designate a point person who can receive historic photos and other material such as books, old films, and antiques from the public. Examples of important historic events might include the arrival of early settlers, the founding of the city, boom and bust cycles, a major fire, or the construction of a new local industry.

Identify suggestions for filming location and scenic background shots. Find a location for conducting interviews that can provide a variety of pleasant backdrops and serve as production headquarters with telephone access. A local museum or home with an impressive lawn and garden might be appropriate. Create a list of favorite places to film scenic backdrops and background footage. If practical, identify volunteers who can assist with special shots, such as those who might own a plane, helicopter, or boat they would be willing to provide for the filming.

Review the edited script and a first cut of the movie. Members of the steering committee should review the script and a first draft or "cut" of the movie for accuracy as well as sensitivity to local issues and people. The time to find a technical mistake or stylistic error takes place well before work on the final version of the video is completed.

Organize the local debut/viewing. Organize an event for the premiere screening of the video. Coordinate with other planning efforts in the community to maximize the impact of the premiere, such as showing the video as part of a communitywide strategic planning session.

Maximize publicity. Develop contacts with local media. Write press releases regarding the filming and the premiere of the video. Think about organizing a press conference at the beginning of the filming and setting up interviews for the media that will take place at the screening.

Identify important roles for volunteers. There are a number of opportunities for local citizens to be involved in the actual shooting of the video. These roles include Co-Producer, Production Coordinator, and Production Assistants. More discussion of possible involvement in these capacities is included in Parts 2, 3, and 4.

Fund-raising. Crucial in any community endeavor, the topic of fund-raising will be addressed in more depth below.

A role for students and teachers. We've found that the most helpful and enthusiastic members of a steering committee are often teachers and students. Audio/video department faculty and staff have provided us with extra equipment and have sometimes become involved in conducting interviews themselves. One high school junior became our official Production Coordinator, efficiently lining up interviews and tracking down extra equipment for us. School gymnasiums and theaters are often the largest public meeting space in town for the screening of the video. It's mutually beneficial to work directly with schools on a production. The involvement of students not only provides the production crew with volunteers, it directly exposes a community's youth—its future leaders—to the issues that a Community Video Project explores.

CREATING THE RIGHT VIDEO

As with any art form, there is no single way to create a Community Video. Ten different videographers all attempting to document a community will end up producing 10 completely different finished products, each with its own emphasis and style. Therefore, it's important during the planning stages of a project for the steering committee to begin thinking about what type of artistic mood and pace might be appropriate in a video about their community.

As explained in Part 3 of this report, interviewing is an art. Here, the authors put an interview subject at ease in an informal setting.

You may want to have the steering committee watch the sample DVD included with this report and analyze what they liked and what they would prefer to change. Are there too many scenes of people talking? Did the video spend an appropriate amount of time on history? On talking to students? Is the music right for your audience? How would you use special effects or graphics to enhance the look of the video?

While the video's editor cannot take into account every person's vision of how the finished piece should look, a general consensus about aesthetic issues should definitely be articulated by the steering committee before editing takes place.

Though the artistic look of each project will vary widely with each community, the basic structure we use is generally the same. It's typically divided into three chronological components.

We've found that the most helpful and enthusiastic members of a steering committee are often teachers and students.

History: the major historical events that have shaped the modern-day character of a community. We suggest focusing on the events that have left a legacy, as well as any unique, amusing, or out-of-the-ordinary moments in local history. In our projects, we have placed particular emphasis on historical events of the twentieth century rather than the distant past because these events are more likely to have had a direct bearing on a community's present-day character.

History is generally comfortable, straightforward, familiar territory to viewers, and it's easy to reflect on in a way that can captivate an audience in the first few minutes of a video. The historical section's liberal use of striking visual images, such as photographs, early maps, old documents, or 1950s-era home movies, will draw in even the most ambivalent of viewers, paving the way for viewers to gradually shift their focus to the present. History can be recounted through narration of historical footage and photographs, and through the stories told by people interviewed for the video.

The modern community: a portrait of a community as it is today. This section can compose the middle section of a video's running time and might begin with a basic overview of a community's various facets: its economic base, employment opportunities, town government, cultural activities, and the quality of its schools, hospitals, public parks, civic organizations, and natural resources.

A video can then delve into an exploration of the present-day community: its strengths and weaknesses, its opportunities and threats. This can be the most complex and controversial section of a video and has the potential to present certain topics that stir or even anger some portion of a community's population. This is inevitable, as every video project will to some extent reflect the perspective of its producers and participants. It is certainly possible and desirable, however, to include many different perspectives on the same topic or issue, creating a sense of balance. Almost all of this section can be told through the voices of people being interviewed.

The future: the many possibilities for the future of a community. This section might incorporate both what citizens predict as the *likely* path they see a community taking, as well as what they *hope* might take place in the future. There's a good chance some of the people you interview have not given the future of your community much thought until you get them in front of the camera. Even more of them will not have discussed their vision for the future with other community members. This is the ultimate reason you want to produce a Community Video: to get people to think about what they can do about the future of their community.

HOW MUCH WILL THE VIDEO COST AND HOW WILL WE PAY FOR IT?

As you prepare to go forward with a Community Video Project, there's probably one question that's been hovering in the back of your mind: how much will this thing cost? Isn't television production supposed to be incredibly expensive? How can I possibly afford to make my video look even remotely professional without having thousands of dollars at my disposal? (That's actually three questions, but who's counting?)

Before you go any further, let us preface the next section with some advice: if you are motivated enough to produce a video about your community, lack of money will not interfere with the project's getting produced. A good producer specializes in being persistent, positive, resourceful, and in creating opportunities out of crisis. There are nearly always opportunities available to borrow a decent camcorder and edit a video at a public access station or school completely free of charge. However, this method of "no-budget" producing can be slow moving, unpolished, and at times a major headache. Having at least a minimal budget will help alleviate some of the strain.

Budgeting a Community Video relies on an accurate assessment of the probable costs incurred during production, while taking into account equipment, staff, and financial resources that are already available. We've put together two potential budget breakdowns detailing moderate and low production budgets. The moderate production budget assumes that key people will be compensated for their time, and that you will be able to use your first choice of high-quality equipment when filming and editing. The low production budget assumes you will make your video on an absolute shoestring, making do with whatever equipment can be borrowed and whatever in-kind services can be provided. All of the elements of each budget are discussed at length below in the major section on production, including a detailed discussion of equipment and editing systems, with references to further information on everything needed to produce a top-quality video project.

We decided not to include a high-end production budget, which would involve hiring a professional production company. If you take this route, the production company you hire will most likely present you with a lump sum, and they will take care of the budget breakdown. As a rule of thumb, video production companies in the year 2001 are likely to charge between $1,000 and $1,500 per finished minute of video. At those rates, your 30-minute documentary would cost between $30,000 and $45,000. Unless you expect to make the next *Blair Witch Project*, we suggest your funds are better spent more sparingly!

Remember that these examples are just sample budgets. Nothing here represents a definitive list of production expenses.

A Moderate Production Budget

The moderate production budget requires roughly $10,000 to $15,000 (again, using dollar figures in the year 2001). This budget will enable video producers to pay for all equipment rentals and supplies, and it will also allow a core staff to receive modest salaries for their labor. While the budget is certainly not extravagant, it is enough to create a professional-looking video product.

This budget should enable you to comfortably produce a polished final product, without cutting any corners or overworking your crew.

A Low Production Budget

It's time to beg, borrow, and steal! Using a low production budget requires you to constantly think on

A MODERATE PRODUCTION BUDGET

EQUIPMENT		
DV camcorder	5 days @$100/day	$500
Lighting kit	5 days @$50/day	250
Tripod	5 days @$25/day	125
Lavolier mike	5 days @$25/day	125
EQUIPMENT TOTAL		**$1,000**
POST-PRODUCTION		
Avid editing suite	7 days @$500/day	$3,500
POST-PRODUCTION TOTAL		**$3,500**
SUPPLIES		
Mini-DV tapes	20 @$15 each	$300
VHS tapes	10 @$5 each	50
Pro halogen bulbs	5 @$20 each	100
VCR	1 @$175	175
Mike batteries	5 @$5/pack	25
Extension cords	2 @$14 each	28
RCA cables	3 @$6 each	18
Pro headphones	1 @$25/set	25
SUPPLIES TOTAL		**$709**
OFFICE		
Phone (including cell phones)		$200
Postage/Fed Ex		50
Miscellaneous (Printer cartridges, paper, internet, etc.)		150
OFFICE TOTAL		**$400**
MISCELLANEOUS		
Gas		$300
Food		1,000
MISCELLANEOUS TOTAL		**$1,200**
Salaries		
Director		$3,000
Producer		2,000
Editor		3,000
Narrator		100
SALARIES TOTAL		**$8,100**
GRAND TOTAL		**$15,009**

your feet. No comfort level is assumed here, and being resourceful is imperative. The low production budget is essentially less than $2,000.

For this type of production, it is advisable to team up with a public access station, high school, or college in your area. Tell the station manager or video instructor about your project and how it directly relates to the community. Offer to give the station or school "production company" credit, free publicity, and most importantly, first opportunity to broadcast the final piece. This can be a tremendous resource for your production. [Note: if your local public access station provides equipment to produce your video, they may require that the station holds copyright to your work.]

Generally, a school or station can provide you with the basics: a Hi-8 or S-VHS camcorder, a Lavolier or shotgun microphone, a tripod, and a lighting kit. You may also have access to a no-frills analogue editing system, although it is now becoming common to find nonlinear, digital editing systems in schools and public stations. If you're lucky enough to get free time on such a system, you can approximate the quality and complexity of a professional editing job.

If you are unable to obtain equipment from a public access station or school, there are other options. You can try borrowing a camcorder from a nonprofit media arts organization, or from a friend or relative. At worst, a decent Hi-8 camcorder costs about $500 these days at the electronics section of any retail store, which also usually sells inexpensive headphones, extension cords, and tripods. A cheap lighting kit can be put together using two or three halogen work lights, which run about $35 each. Some electronics stores carry cheap Lavolier and shotgun mikes for less than $50. For an editing system, try purchasing low-cost editing software for your home computer (more on this in Part 4). If all else fails for editing facilities, you can always hook up two VCRs and transfer each clip by hitting "pause" and "record."

We have two suggestions before you race ahead with this budget. First of all, if a borrowed tripod doesn't deliver smooth tilts and pans, it's worth the small amount

A LOW PRODUCTION BUDGET

EQUIPMENT

Hi-8 camcorder	borrowed ($500 to buy)	0-$500
Halogen work lights	borrowed ($100 to buy)	0-$100
Tripod	borrowed ($100 to rent or buy)	0-$100
Lavolier mike	borrowed ($50 to buy)	0-$50
VCR	borrowed ($100 to buy)	0-$100
Extension cords	borrowed ($30 to buy)	0-$30
RCA cables	borrowed ($15 to buy)	0-$15
Headphones	borrowed ($20 to buy)	0-$20
	EQUIPMENT TOTAL	**0-$915**

SUPPLIES

Hi-8 tapes	8 @ $10 each	$80
VHS tapes	10 @ $5 each	50
3/4" u-matic tapes (analog edits only)	2 @ $25 each	50
	SUPPLIES TOTAL	**$130-180**

POST-PRODUCTION (3 OPTIONS)

(1) public access / school editing suite (Hi-8 to 3/4" u-matic system)	borrowed	0
(2) nonlinear editing system	borrowed	0
(3) nonlinear editing software (Requires proper computer—see Part 4)		$500
	POST-PRODUCTION TOTAL	**0-$500**

MISCELLANEOUS

Gas		$100
Food (includes donations from local restaurants)		300
Phone and office		100
	MISCELLANEOUS TOTAL	**$500**

GRAND TOTAL $630–$2095

of money it costs to rent a more professional tripod or to buy a decent one at a retail store. This can vastly improve the look of your video, and it will make the process much easier, especially when taping extreme close-up pans on historical photographs.

The second suggestion is: never let your crew go hungry! When people aren't being paid to work on a production, the one compensation they have to look forward to is a good meal on the set or in the office. Even pizza, subs, or donuts can cheer up a hardworking crew. If you're on a micro-budget, try to approach local restaurants about donating one or two meals to the crew in exchange for credit in the documentary.

In conclusion, the message for this budget is: scrounge!

Fund-raising

No matter how much you're willing to spend to produce a Community Video Project, there will always be some degree of fund-raising or resource-gathering involved. For the sake of clarity, we want to divide fund-raising into two categories: money and in-kind donations. In-kind contributions are frequently offered in lieu of hard cash, and are often as valuable as cash in a given situation. Free use of a nonlinear editing system or professional video camera, or donated time from a professional editor or video producer, would be directly equal in value to the cash required to pay for these expensive production elements. Free food from a restaurant, use of an office's phones, and the services of production volunteers are also good in-kind contributions

The first rule in fund-raising is to be sure you know what you're doing. Clearly outline the purpose and goals of the project, the activities you need to carry out, and the expected budget you will require. Then we recommend assigning one or more members of the steering committee the responsibility of raising money and procuring in-kind resources, such as equipment and volunteers.

The places you may be able to find cash funds for your project are the local planning commission or town/city/county government, charitable foundations, local businesses and civic organizations, and individuals who are excited about the project. Also keep in mind that whenever you receive in-kind donations of equipment or volunteer time, it will directly affect your bottom line and reduce your need to raise hard cash.

Local planning commission or town/city/county government. Many local governments have funds that can be used for planning purposes, although this varies widely from place to place. Your Community Video Project can clearly be considered a visioning document that would provide planning benefits to your community. The planning commission may have access to special regional or state planning funds that can be procured for the project. Your local government may also contribute to the project through its general funds.

Foundations. There are thousands of charitable grant-making foundations throughout the United States. Most geographic areas are served by a special type of foundation, called a "community foundation," that often serves as a clearinghouse for several philanthropic funds. Community foundations usually have general grants programs for a wide variety of community projects. Some communities have charitable endowments set up specifically to do community projects. The two best pieces of advice we can give you regarding grants from foundations follow.

Do your research. Your task is to do the research to find a foundation focused in your geographic area and interested in community development, planning, or local video production. Never make a

The first rule in fund-raising is to be sure you know what you're doing.

SOURCES OF FUNDING FOR ONE PROJECT

Local community foundation:	$4,000 grant ($5,000 request)
Individuals on steering committee:	$800 (10 contributors)
Civic organizations:	$300 (3 organizations)
Businesses (including 3 banks):	$900
Total	**$6,000**

Many local businesses have an interest in doing something good for the community as well as cultivating good public relations.

grant application to a foundation with no interest in your project. As one foundation staff person put it, "I often wonder if these same people try to buy their groceries in hardware stores." The most comprehensive source for charitable foundation information is *The Foundation Directory*, published by the Foundation Center (www.fdncenter.org). At about $300, we don't recommend you buy the book, but you can find it at most major libraries. You can also access the Foundation Center's on-line database (www.fdncenter.org/marketplace/index.html) for a fee of $29.95 per month. It's well worth the cost if your trip to the nearest major library is over an hour's drive away.

Follow the guidelines. When you find a foundation you believe would be interested in your video project, call and ask for their grant guidelines. Most foundations have specific guidelines that tell you what the foundation is interested in, proposal deadline dates, how much to ask for, and the specific format your proposal should follow. *Follow these guidelines when you write your grant proposal.* Be clear about the benefits you expect to provide the community and present a responsible budget. It is always useful to disclose if others have invested time or money in this project. If you need further assistance writing a grant proposal, we recommend *Grassroots Grants* by Andy Robinson (1996) This is the source of the above quote about hardware stores.

One other note: Foundations make grants only to tax-exempt IRS 501(c)(3) charitable organizations or to public agencies and governments. You may need your local government or a 501(c)(3) organization, such as a local historical society, to make the grant application at your request.

Local businesses. Many local businesses have an interest in doing something good for the community as well as cultivating good public relations. Focus on the good that the donation to the video project will do for the community, as well as the marketing benefits to the business of being included in the credits at the end of the video. Prepare a written proposal and responsible budget that you can leave with the business. In the best case scenario, recruit an individual who has a good relationship with the business to make the request with you. If your video is broadcast on a local cable public access channel, you can precede or follow the video with a "Made possible with generous support by . . ." underwriter message. Keep in mind that although public broadcasting stations also use these messages, the money raised is to cover the cost of broadcasting the video, and not necessarily to cover your costs of producing the video.

Individuals. One of the advantages of having a broad-based steering committee is that you generate excitement among many people who can make small donations to the project. It is not unreasonable for people of modest means to contribute $100 if they believe in what you are doing. Others might have access to matching or small grants funds through their employers, or they may be associated with organizations, such as the chamber of commerce or the historical society, that can afford a modest contribution. There are a few individuals of significant means who make choices every day regarding charitable contributions. Get them excited about the project and tell them how they can help.

Stretching dollars. Whatever method you use to raise funds, you can make each dollar you spend go a long way if you are resourceful, especially in your search for equipment. Shop around extensively, and if you are on a tight budget, never pay the first price you are quoted. Equipment rental houses are used to dealing with professional producers for whom haggling is imperative, so working to get a discount or package deal is integral to the process of renting equipment. Sometimes a rental house will give a four-day price for a week's rental or will throw in sound or lighting kits with a camera at no extra cost. This pertains especially to lining up an editing system and professional editor, both of which can be very expensive at market value.

Student volunteers. Many high schools and colleges will offer students some form of course credit if the students volunteer on a public service project. A Community Video Project is a great learning experience for students interested in film, broadcast, or communications studies, and many will jump at the chance to gain valuable experience and school credit by working on a real production.

By now you should have the following essentials in place:

- a steering committee comprised of a wide variety of community members
- locations and people to interview identified
- a budget
- financing

You now need to put together your equipment, your production crew, and your production headquarters. For these, we'll move on to Part Two.

PART 2

Pre-production: Equipment and Scheduling

Before you can begin shooting a Community Video Project, you'll need to carry out a number of tasks. Specifically, you will need to:

- arrange all necessary resources, including equipment, locations, and staff;

- conduct proper research on the community, its history, its residents, and its issues;

- arrange interviews and schedule all aspects of the video production; and

- establish advance publicity to get word out about the production.

Let's begin by discussing the equipment you'll need. Remember, this is only the most basic list necessary to produce a quality Community Video. You may want to examine further options using the references included at the end of this section.

EQUIPMENT YOU'LL NEED
Video Cameras
In a perfect world, we would use the same Beta-SP or Digital Beta cameras used by professional television networks. This is a surefire way to guarantee that your production will be shot in a high-resolution medium that is suitable for broadcast on a major television network like PBS. Unfortunately, these cameras are prohibitively expensive and require special skills to operate. They are also very big and heavy, and use special tapes and playback decks that are neither affordable nor available to the average consumer. In Fruita, Colorado, we arranged a partnership with a regional PBS station and its cameraman to use such equipment, saving us a great deal of money on professional camera rentals and creating a video that was broadcast-ready for television. The evidence is contained on the DVD that you'll find inside the back cover of this report. For all other projects, in which having a broadcast-ready format was less of an issue, we successfully used a more reasonable, yet high-quality, alternative: Mini-DV.

A Mini-DV or Digital Video camera has been the central piece of equipment for our Community Video Projects because it's (1) high-quality, (2) nonthreatening, (3) very portable, and (4) affordable. Mini-DV was introduced for consumer use around 1995 and is now offered by all major camera manufacturers.

The "Mini" in this case implies that the camera uses tiny digital tapes that cost $12 to $22, as opposed to a professional digital camera like DVC-Pro, which uses larger tapes that cost $70 or more. Mini-DV cameras cost from $1,000 to $5,000, with subtle variations in quality and performance throughout that range. What you get is twice the resolution of a VHS camcorder, CD-quality audio, amazing low-light capability, super-high color saturation, and special cables that allow you to download your footage as binary computer code straight into a hard drive. You can also make unlimited generations of copies from an original tape with absolutely no loss of quality. Rental equipment houses offer package deals on Mini-DV cameras at very good rates.

Sometimes cost, timing, and availability will get the best of you. Although it's the preferred option, you don't need a Mini-DV camera to shoot a great Community Video. Super VHS and Hi 8 cameras use two video formats that are still relatively high quality, and they're very easy to find and less expensive to buy or rent.

Tripods

A tripod will help you compose a terrific array of stylish shots, including smooth panning shots from side to side and fluid upward and downward tilt shots. For most interviews, location work, and historical footage, a tripod is an absolute necessity. Shaky, erratic camera work can ruin an otherwise great sequence on tape.

Just like cameras, tripods come in different styles, varying in quality and ranging in price from less than $100 to many hundreds of dollars. We suggest you try to borrow one from a local school or cable-access TV station, as these places tend to stock better tripods that will stand up to repeated heavy use. In rental situations, you can usually get a good tripod along with a camera as a package. A decent, inexpensive tripod can be purchased at most electronics stores or any place that cameras are sold. We strongly suggest using a tripod that has a fluid, fully adjustable head. This will help make your camera work look as professional as possible, especially for smooth pans.

A word about broadcast quality . . .

If your Community Video is not intended for broadcast on network television, Mini-DV should suffice very well in terms of visual quality and resolution, even for small local cable-access stations. However, if your community is determined to pitch its project to a major television station, you will need to consider working with a professional video production company that can help you find the right equipment and operator to ensure that the finished project is suitable for major broadcast. You will also want to contact television stations in your community's area before shooting your project to determine what will be required in terms of quality. Also, arrangements might be made with stations like PBS to co-produce the Community Video and thus reduce your community's expenses. Remember, while major broadcast is a nice bonus, the real point of a Community Video is to get your community together to think about the future, so killing yourself to do a broadcast-ready production may involve more than your community needs.

Our favorite Mini-DV Cameras . . .

As you'll see, we're a little partial to Sony and Canon, the unofficial favorites among independent film makers and Web-content creators. We've described a mix of cameras, ranging in retail price from around $700 to $4,000. In April 2001, the time at which the final edit of this report was taking place, all four of these cameras were highly regarded in the world of videography for solid combinations of features, performance, and overall value.

Since the prices and functionality of equipment such as cameras can change very rapidly, you may want to do additional research before committing to buy. You may also want to learn more about the detailed technical features of various cameras. Please consult Appendix B of this report, which includes website and telephone contact information for numerous camera manufacturers. This information can be helpful in making technical decisions about which camera to buy.

Sony DCR–VX 1000. **Advantages:** This camera's size allows for steady shots in locations work; it also boasts a powerful zoom lens. **Features:** Audio-level meter, tape counter, and battery-level readouts on the back panel. This was the first consumer market digital camcorder and to this day it's still a popular, high-quality option. Durable and reliable with great results.

Sony DCR-TRV900. **Advantages:** This unit's small size makes it easy to set up on a tripod, frame shots, and take awkward angle shots. **Features**: Pop-out LCD screen, still-photo button. A great little DV camcorder that won't break your budget but still outperforms many larger cameras.

Canon XL1. **Advantages:** This semi-pro camera has instantly adjustable aperture and gain settings, with a top-quality interchangeable lens system. **Features:** Interchangeable Canon fluorite lens, shotgun microphone, large eyepiece. This camcorder is the top choice in its price range among serious professionals. Expensive but unbeatable in its price range for quality.

Canon GL1. **Advantages:** A smaller, cheaper version of the XL1, also with top performance for its price range. **Features:** Pop-out color LCD viewfinder, adjustable iris, Canon fluorite lens. Probably the highest-rated small camcorder on the market.

Careful with that tripod! . . .

As with light stands and any other tall, awkward, fragile apparatus that supports an expensive piece of equipment, be careful about how and where you set up your tripod. Make certain that all three legs and the head are locked in place before you walk away from it. Extension cords are a tripod's natural enemy and will insidiously attempt to wrap themselves around a tripod's legs and coerce an idle passerby into snagging them, bringing your production to a crashing halt. Try "sandbagging" your tripod by hanging a heavy knapsack or plastic shopping bag from the middle of the leg brace. It may save your camera.

Microphones

All Mini-DV cameras and consumer camcorders come with built-in microphones. Trust us: none of them are worth using alone to record sound on a Community Video Project. The built-in mikes that come with all cameras are "omni-directional" and are intended to efficiently capture sound from all points around the camera. Don't rely on the camera mike unless you want your video to pick up sounds even a German Shepherd can't hear.

To get professional sound you will learn to love a tiny little microphone. It's called a Lavolier microphone (the lav). It's the only mike you'll ever really need for documentary interviews and good directional sound. Like any external microphone, the lav can be plugged into your camera's "microphone input" jack. Once plugged in, the lav immediately replaces the inferior built-in mike.

The basic lav consists of a raisin-sized microphone, connected by a long cord to a big metal plug that houses an AA battery and has an on/off switch. The plug end of the lav goes into an adapter on your camera, and the microphone clips onto your subject's lapel, shirt pocket, tie—near enough to the subject's chest to pick up vocal resonance. The lav should also come with a little foam screen that shields the mike from wind and outdoor noise. Wireless lavs will give you more freedom of movement for "walk and talk" interviews, such as when a person is showing you a local landmark or walking you through a historic building or district. Wireless lavs are also notorious for running out of battery power. Wireless or not, be sure to stock lots of extra batteries for any lav you intend to use. We recommend buying one of the battery brands that come with a little power tester on the package; that way you can test your lav batteries before each interview and save yourself the grief of a ruined interview.

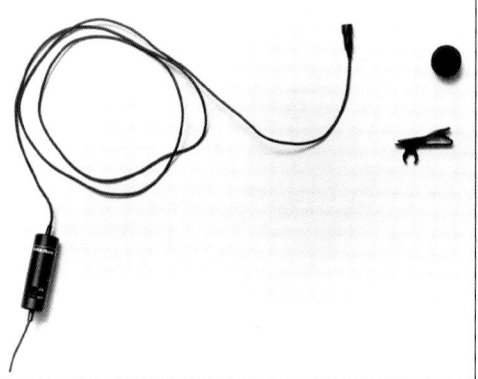

The Lavolier microphone is easy to work with. Wireless lavs are available that allow an interview subject to "walk and talk," but beware the draining power on batteries of a wireless lav.

Headphones

Speaking of ruined interviews, if you're not monitoring your sound through the camera, chances are you won't notice when something's not right. For this reason, a headphone set is an essential companion to your microphone. By plugging it into the headphone jack on your camera, you can accurately adjust the audio level coming in from the mike, and update the level through the course of an interview if it is uneven. You can also get a good initial feel for how the mike is placed on the subject and pick up little quirks that the naked ear misses, which become disasters when you finish taping and play back the results. You hear exactly what the mike hears, so there's nothing left to chance.

A good set of headphones costs less than $20 and can be purchased at any electronics store. We highly recommend the home-stereo kind with large pads that cover the ears, rather than walkman-type headphones.

Quality stereo headphones usually come with quarter-inch plugs, which require an adapter to fit into the small walkman-sized jack on your camera. Many of these headphones come with adapters, but make certain you have one or can get one in the same store before buying the headphones.

Headphones are vital to making sure that you are getting a recording that is useable. Headphones that fully cover the ear, rather than Walkman headphones, are preferable.

Lighting Kits

While professional lighting kits are not cheap to buy, they can often be borrowed or rented from a public access station, college media-services department, or photographic studio. A good lighting kit will lend a look and feel of professionalism to your production and will include everything you need to light masterfully. It's great to be able to develop your own lighting techniques using good equipment.

A standard lighting kit generally comes with three lights and three accompanying light stands. Most of the individual lights will come with "barn doors," which are side and top flaps that allow you to increase or decrease the amount of light hitting your subject. Lighting kits also usually contain reflector boards. These boards are especially useful for outdoor shooting. One side of the board is shiny, the other is white. The reflector board's shiny side is great for eliminating dark shadows on your interview subject by reflecting the sun's rays. The plain white side is good for creating subtle shadows to soften overly bright sun rays.

A good lighting kit will add a feel of professionalism to your production. Here, the authors light an interview with a local priest.

 **PART 2 HIGHLIGHTS**

Pre-production: Equipment and scheduling . . .

- Mini DV cameras open up the opportunity for local videographers to produce high-quality video at a reasonable price.

- The main equipment items you will need are:
    1. video camera;
    2. tripod;
    3. Lavolier microphone;
    4. headphones;
    5. lighting kit;
    6. cables;
    7. extension cords and power strips;
    8. batteries and battery charger;
    9. duct tape or gaffer's tape; and
    10. reflector board.

    All of these can be rented from supply houses or found locally.

- Choose a base of operations that has:
    1. a nice variety of backdrops for outdoor and indoor interviews;
    2. access to phone lines, photocopy and fax machines, e-mail, and electrical outlets;
    3. space for morning production meetings; and
    4. is centrally located and easy for residents to find.

- The production crew will include:
    1. a camera operator;
    2. a sound operator;
    3. a production coordinator;
    4. production assistants;
    5. an editor;
    6. a writer; and
    7. a narrator.

- Historical research should include:
    1. a historical time line with key events;
    2. historical photographs;
    3. maps, documents, paintings;
    4. home movies; and
    5. pre-arranged interviews with older citizens, local historians, or anyone who can relate colorful anecdotes about local history.

- Conduct a publicity campaign for the video shoot to let the community know what you are up to and why.

- Schedule interviews, select scenic backdrops around town to film "B-roll" (see page 30), and compile a list of other photogenic community events for you to capture on video.

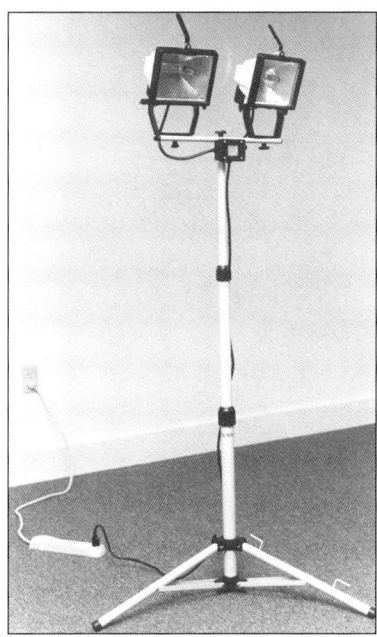

A very effective and cost-efficient alternative to a pro lighting kit can be purchased at most hardware stores in the form of halogen-quartz (not incandescent or fluorescent) shop lights. You can buy halogen shop lights that come with stands which set up easily. On our Swanton, Vermont, shoot we bought three sets of twin 500-watt halogen lamps, mounted together on a big, sturdy, metal telescoping stand with great lock rings. These three units gave us a total of 3,000 watts of brilliant white halogen light, easily comparable to what a professional kit delivers, for a total of $108 plus tax. Not bad. And, as you'll see on the enclosed DVD, the Swanton video came out looking very good.

While you're in the store, pick up a piece of white foam core board or a reflective auto windshield sunscreen. These work great as homemade reflector boards. If you're in a pinch and nothing else is available, tape sheets of aluminum foil or white paper to a nice big piece of cardboard. Sunlight will very happily bounce off these inexpensive surfaces.

Reflector boards are used to direct the sunlight in ways that will enhance your shots.

Beware the heat of halogen lights . . .

Halogen lights get extremely hot. Be very careful around them and make certain that their power cords don't run across places where passers-by, animals, or children can trip on them and pull them over. The higher you raise the lighting stands, the more easily they fall over, so for added security we hang heavy knapsacks or plastic shopping bags from the bases of the stands for ballast. Be very, very aware of how close your lights are to flammable surfaces and objects. On one interview we noticed a smoking curtain just before the halogen lamp six inches away ignited it completely. Burning down a historical society is not a great way to positively motivate a community.

Halogen lights need time to cool down before they can be dismantled and packed up for the next location. Take the cool-down process into account when you schedule your interviews—about 20 minutes. When you do burn out a bulb and have to replace it, do not touch the new bulb with your bare fingers; the oil from your fingers will cause it to shatter when it heats up.

Cables

The cables that come with the camera you rent or buy will usually be shorter than you want or insufficient for your plans to take the camera into your community. Cables and cable adapters are what hold all your equipment together. We suggest you stock up on the following.

RCA cables: The RCA is the basic cable that comes with all stereos, VCRs, and video cameras. While all of these appliances use the same type of RCA plug for input and output, the RCA cable for a camera will specifically have three plugs on each end: red for Left Audio, white for Right Audio, and black/yellow for Video. You may notice that the RCA-cable video jack on your camera is officially called the "Composite Video Output" because it combines both the luminance (light and dark) and the chrominance (colors) of your video image into one signal.

The longer the camera RCA cable, the better. Six feet or longer is good. It's also not a bad idea to have a couple of extra three-plug or even two-plug

RCA cables on hand. They're cheap and can be found at any store that sells video or electronics components. Pick up an "RCA to Coaxial Cable" adapter in case you find you want to hook up your camera to an old TV.

S-VIDEO cables: If you're shooting your Community Video Project in a hi-band format, such as Mini-DV, Hi-8, or S-VHS, the only way to actually see the benefits of the higher resolution on a monitor is to use an S-VIDEO cable rather than an RCA cable. The S-VIDEO cable is capable of carrying a higher-quality image than RCA because an S-VIDEO jack splits the luminance and chrominance of the video image into two signals. While RCA cables are more convenient for simply viewing your footage, S-VIDEO cables are especially important for making high-quality transfers and copies of your footage. Unless you're using Firewire (see the next paragraph), definitely use an S-VIDEO cable to transfer footage, so that the highest possible resolution is carried into a recording deck or editing computer.

Firewire cables: One of the most impressive aspects of the Mini-DV format lies in its ability to encode video images as binary code. With Mini-DV, you can make a copy of a copy of a copy *ad infinitum* and never lose any resolution.

To accommodate this miraculous transfer of digital information, most good Mini-DV cameras have special input/output ports for a cable called "firewire." This cable will convey the digital signal straight out of a Mini-DV camera into a digital recording deck, another DV camera, or a computer—strictly as binary code. Firewire cables can be expensive but are well worth the quality.

Extension Cords and Power Strips
You can never have too much power. Most of the time you'll be using three halogen lights, a camera, a battery charger, and a monitor, all of which have three-prong plugs. A three-prong to two-prong plug adapter, a 50-foot long industrial extension cord, and a six-plug power strip will fill these power requirements very well. You may even consider getting two adapters, two extension cords, and two power strips. Make sure all your cords and power strips are suitable for use outdoors.

Camera Batteries
Your camera is a huge power hog. Every clever little function built into the camera uses energy. Standby Mode, Lens Zoom, and Tape Eject are just a few of your battery's biggest drains. Aside from their high price, camera batteries need frequent charging, and Community Video Projects demand constant mobility. Always stock an adequate supply of charged batteries so you can capture on-the-street footage or driving sequences without running low on camera power. When the camera isn't being used, the batteries should be charging. You never know when the best interview you ever get will be on a sidewalk, far away from an extension cord.

Tape
You'll be using it for everything from taping down loose extension cords to strapping extra cables and camera batteries to your tripod. Duct tape sticks to one thing better than anything else—itself, especially when wet. For a tape that has a stickier surface for things like carpets and wood, we sometimes use gaffer's tape instead of duct tape, especially when we get it for free. Professional lighting people and movie electricians absolutely insist on gaffer's tape, which is very strong black cloth tape, and it sticks to anything and everything, unlike its cheaper relative. It's not as easy to find and it's fairly expensive, but if you have it, use it.

EQUIPMENT CHECKLIST

Before you plunge into Production, let's go over the checklist one more time:

- ❏ Video Camera
- ❏ Tripod
- ❏ Lavolier Microphone
- ❏ Headphones
- ❏ Lighting Kit
- ❏ Cables
- ❏ Extension Cords and Power Strips
- ❏ Batteries and Battery Charger
- ❏ Duct tape or Gaffer's tape
- ❏ Reflector Board

You never have too much power or too many extension cords and connector sites.

The first thing to line up before you start scheduling interviews is a central location that you can use as a base of operations during the shoot.

SELECTING AN INTERVIEW LOCATION

Now that you've managed to wrangle all of the proper equipment, you're ready to start scheduling the logistics of the shoot. The first thing to line up before you start scheduling interviews is a central location that you can use as a base of operations during the shoot. This should be a location that can serve both as a "set" and a production office.

We have found that a highly efficient way to capture a large number of interviews is to ask people being interviewed to come to our "Community Video Headquarters" instead of our having to drive to their homes or offices. Centralizing the interviews in one or two convenient locations allows us to dramatically decrease our equipment set-up time. We are able to leave our camcorders and lights in place as we wait for each person to arrive. If you're doing most of your interviews outside, you can eliminate the lighting setup and do more interviews on the run.

In Morristown, Vermont, we used virtually one location for all our interviews, although this can often lead to repetitive backgrounds. In Fruita, Colorado, two locations sufficed nicely, especially since everything was shot outside in the Colorado sunlight without extra lights. In Swanton, Vermont, we used one location for a while and then abandoned it in favor of rapidly scheduled interviews wherever we happened to be. The Fruita and Swanton videos can be viewed on the DVD that is included in this report. You'll find a system that works best for you.

An ideal base of operations provides:

- a nice variety of backdrops for outdoor and indoor interviews;
- access to phone lines, photocopy and fax machines, e-mail, and electrical outlets;
- space for morning production meetings; and
- a central location that is easy for residents to find.

ASSEMBLING THE PRODUCTION CREW

With your base of operations in place, you now need to assemble the main staff of people who will work on the production. The "crew" consists of a number of people filling clearly defined roles, serving both on the set and in the office. Below are some brief job descriptions for each crew member needed; many of these roles can be combined, such as camera/sound operator or production coordinator/manager. Be certain that each crew

The Swanton Library: a good kind of place for an interview . . .

The Library in Swanton is a newly refurbished nineteenth century building, located directly on the green at the center of Swanton Village. The library has three floors offering a variety of interview settings, including the village green for outdoor interviews. The Swanton Historical Society is also located right in the basement, with easy equipment access via elevator. Phone, e-mail/Internet access, and photocopy and fax machines are available on site. Coffee and morning pastries are just across the street.

member is suited for the role that has been assigned. You can learn more about the technical detail of these roles by consulting the references listed in Appendix B of this report.

Camera operator. This person is in charge of focusing, lighting, and framing shots, and taking general responsibility for the camera. The camera operator should have a good eye as well as a working knowledge of camera techniques, such as getting the critical focus, setting the white balance, creating good composition of still and moving shots, and labeling and storing finished tapes.

Two good sources of information for camera work are *Desktop Digital Video Production* by Frederick Jones (McGraw-Hill, 1998), and *The Complete Idiot's Guide to Making Home Videos* by Steven Beal (Alpha Books, 2000).

Sound operator. This important role is usually the responsibility of the camera operator. The sound operator places the lav microphone on each interview subject and listens to each interview through the camcorder headphones to determine if there are distracting noises in the background, such as a plane flying overhead. The sound operator adjusts the audio input levels on the camcorder accordingly.

Production coordinator. The production coordinator is critical to the production. This person is in charge of creating the day-to-day time and location schedule for the whole production. The production coordinator begins working in pre-production by telephoning potential interviewees from a phone list and filling in a calendar with time slots during which each person can be interviewed. The production coordinator is also responsible for reminding each interviewee of the scheduled interview; scheduling B-roll (non-interview) footage to be shot at various locations, scheduling the taping of particular activities and events in town, and tracking all other production activities to ensure smooth operations. The production coordinator also fields phone calls at the production office during the days of shooting, rearranging, canceling, and adding interviews to the schedule as the production progresses.

Production manager. The production manager is the main person in charge of overseeing the production. In most cases, this person will probably be you. The production manager is responsible for arranging equipment pickup and drop-off, providing guidance to other crew members, and meeting and chatting with the interviewees as they arrive. The production manager will probably also be conducting the interviews. The documentary's production manager is like the captain of a ship; he or she must steer the project through the storm. When the production manager is also involved in the actual filming, such as providing guidance to the camera and sound crew, the production manager can also be considered the director.

Production assistants. No movie set would be complete without production assistants. These crew members make sure essential things get done. The production assistants are responsible for picking up extra tapes or equipment, carrying around equipment and helping to assemble lights, electrical cables and tripods on the set, running out to buy snacks and meals for the rest of the crew, and helping tear down and pack away equipment at the end of a shoot.

A good place to recruit production assistants might be a local high school or community college, where one might find enthusiastic students eager to help out on an actual video production. It may be preferable to have a "rotating schedule" for production assistants, allowing each PA to work only one or two days. This will ensure that the production assistants remain fresh and energetic and don't get burned out.

The camera operator needs a working knowledge of camera techniques, including getting critical focus, white balance, and good composition.

The production coordinator is responsible for scheduling of all aspects of the video shoot.

> *Next to production itself, editing has the biggest impact on the final outcome of a video project.*

Editor. Although the editor (unless it's you) won't begin working until production is finished, this person is extremely important to the project and should be lined up well in advance. Next to production itself, editing has the biggest impact on the final outcome of a video project. Make sure you find an editor who will be willing to work within your budget. If possible, find an editor who can also provide or help find an editing system on which to work. Taking the time to arrange for editing before production will be extremely helpful!

We cannot emphasize enough the importance of finding a competent editor and using decent editing equipment to produce a quality Community Video. As this report is being written, many new software products are becoming available at reasonable prices that will enable lay people to successfully edit video content. However, editing is as much art as science, so a thorough review of good editing techniques is highly recommended.

One good guide to editing is *Nonlinear Editing Basics: Electronic Film and Video Editing* by Steven E. Brown (Focal Press, 1998). Two good online sources for Digital Video Editing on the web can be found at www.digitalvideoediting.com and at www.nonlinear3.com

Writer. Although much of the video will use the voices of people in your community to tell the community's story, you will need a writer to create clear narration for the video. The writer's script will tell the history of the community and provide transition between different topics and interviews in the video.

Narrator. The narrator will read the video script. The narrator should be someone with a distinctive, professional voice. Be sure the narrator knows the correct pronunciation of local place names and other locally distinctive words.

HISTORICAL RESEARCH

Before production begins, it is important to do extensive historical research so that you have a clear picture in your head of the visual images that might accompany the historical narration. There should be one full day set aside for gathering and recording historical images, and it's highly advisable to make a list of a community's major historical events before searching for these images. Having a working knowledge of a community's history is also very helpful when leading discussions with interview subjects.

Outlining Major Historical Events

Get together with members of the historical society or hunt down any printed information that exists about a community's history in books, magazine and newspaper articles, brochures, or essays. Then leaf through these documents and condense them into a rudimentary historical time line of the major community events over the years.

As a general rule, first and foremost try to include the events that have had a significant role in shaping the modern-day character of a community. Amusing or out-of-the-ordinary anecdotes can also help show the unique character of a town.

Sources of Historical Information and Photographs

Actual images of historic events will bring your community's history to life in the video. Work closely with your local historical society or other history buffs to locate old photographs, maps, documents, newspaper headlines, and even film footage. There may even be a source of film

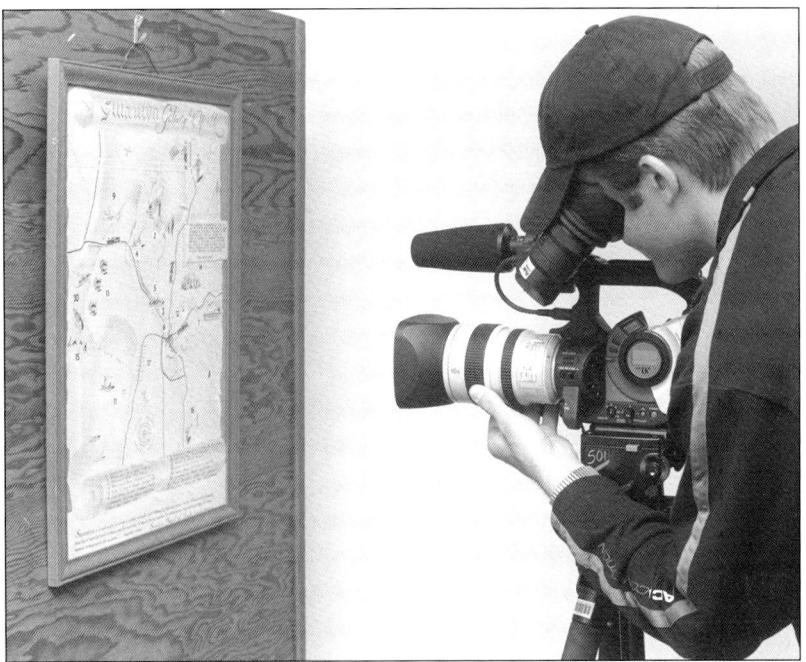

History is a very important part of any Community Video Project. Find and capture dramatic and important images from the community's past.

 **HISTORY CHECKLIST**

Here's a checklist of all the elements you need in Pre-Production for the historical section:

❏ The historical time line with key events

❏ Historical photographs

❏ Maps, documents, paintings

❏ Home movies

❏ Pre-arranged interviews with older citizens, local historians, or anyone who can relate colorful anecdotes about local history

about a region. For instance, Northeast Historic Film in Bucksport, Maine, (www.oldfilm.org) has an inventory of preserved moving picture images of Northern New England and a searchable database. If an official history has been written of the community, use it. For recent events, contact the local television stations to see if they have archival footage. Put out the call in the community for old home movies and photos. The pictures local citizens find are likely to be less formal and more candid than the public photographs at the historical society. If you are unable to have home movie footage professionally transferred to video, just videotape the projected images off the wall of a darkened room.

Libraries or town offices will often have priceless maps, documents, or photos that are framed under glass on the wall. If possible, attempt to get permission to remove the document from the glass while taping.

Photos can also be downloaded from the Internet as JPEG files and then imported directly into a digital editing system's clip library, eliminating the need to videotape them. Scanning old photographs is another quick way of capturing an image in a computer. This is the preferred method, and it will save you a great deal of time and effort. In place of using a camera to painstakingly capture photos on tape, editing software such as *Adobe After Effects* can create computerized pans and zooms of scanned images far more smoothly than any human camera operator.

Once you've compiled a wide array of historical photographs, start going through them to narrow down those to be used for the video. Set aside any photographs showing familiar areas in a town that have changed drastically since the photo was taken. Include photos that clearly establish the mood of the era in which they were taken. For the 1880s, it might be people traveling by train or horse and cart. For the 1920s, it could be a couple driving their first automobile. Look for lively shots of residents in recognizable settings, perhaps involved in activities that still take place.

Put out the call in the community for old home movies and photos. The pictures local citizens find are likely to be less formal and more candid than the public photographs at the historical society.

Using a megaphone is certainly not the most efficient way of getting the word out. Instead, use press releases and an organized publicity campaign, including your own press conference.

PUBLICITY: GETTING THE WORD OUT

Before the first day of shooting approaches, it's time to get the word out around town about the production. This "pre-production publicity campaign" will accomplish a number of goals:

1. It will psychologically prepare people in town to be interviewed and taped on camera in public.

2. It will help pave the way for getting post-production facilities for free or for a discount.

3. It will set the stage for more publicity when the video is done and the premiere screening is being organized.

The most efficient and professional way to get publicity is to write up and send out a press release. This is a brief summary used to convey important points of information about a project to the media. Keep in mind that most local media will have deadlines. If you have a weekly paper, be sure you send them a press release well in advance of their weekly deadline, usually two days before production.

Here are some useful ideas to help you compose a press release.

1. Start your press release with the phrase: "FOR IMMEDIATE RELEASE" followed by the date you plan to fax it out to the media. This is publicity lingo for "URGENT." Then on the next line, put the text: "FOR FURTHER INFORMATION CONTACT:" followed by your name, phone number, and e-mail address.

2. Begin your press release with a punchy "teaser" line, such as "It's happening," or "The wait is over." If nothing else, this will get rid of writer's block.

3. The most attention-getting part of any sentence should be put at the *beginning*, not buried in the middle or the end. An example of this would be: "SWANTON is about the become the star of its own documentary video." *Always* try to begin each paragraph with a word or name that instantly grabs people's attention.

4. Keep your sentences and paragraphs extremely short. Paragraphs should never be more than four lines.

5. Whenever you mention a crucial point that you want readers to remember, put it in ALL CAPITALS or even **CAPITALS WITH BOLDFACE**.

6. Limit your press release to a single page.

Start a publicity campaign by approaching local print and broadcast media; often someone in your community will have contacts at local newspapers, radio stations, and TV stations. Phone the contacts first, then fax them copies of the press release. Be certain to follow up with phone calls to ensure your faxes were received and to find out if and when news of the project will be announced. You can even schedule a press conference as part of your activities during the first day of shooting. For groups who meet regularly, be sure they have information on the Video Project to announce at their meetings. Offer to make a presentation.

A very effective way to spread the word is e-mail. Have residents and local organizations forward a brief description of the project through their e-mail contacts.

SCHEDULING THE SHOOT
Arranging Interviews

It is now the all-important job of the production coordinator to get on the phone and spend a couple of days tracking down people to be interviewed. After all, without interviews, there's no Community Video.

The steering committee should have already developed a list of potential interviewees with a broad range of backgrounds. The production coordinator should ideally be someone who personally knows and is known by many of the prospective interview subjects. The production coordinator should also be able to employ a warm, personable approach over the phone when "cold calling" strangers, projecting an enthusiasm about the project that will inspire people to participate. Don't be overly pushy; if someone is camera shy or too busy to do an interview, just move to the next person on the call list.

As the production coordinator contacts each person, a production calendar should be used to mark the dates and times of each interview. This calendar will be used as the basis for the production schedule sheets. One hour between interviews is more than sufficient if the interviews are being conducted in one place.

Compiling a List of Local Events

Once all the interviews are in place on the production calendar, the production coordinator should compile a list of interesting local events that take place during the days or weeks of the shoot. Public events are a great way to visually establish community life. They create a nice variation from standard interview footage and landscape footage that would otherwise dominate the video. Typical weekly events such as local government meetings, Little League games, bingo

---

**PRESS RELEASE FOR THE
SWANTON, VERMONT, COMMUNITY VIDEO**

FOR IMMEDIATE RELEASE:
JUNE 1, 2000

FOR FURTHER INFORMATION CONTACT:
CABOT ORTON OR RON KILBURN

SWANTON TO BE SUBJECT OF ORTON FAMILY FOUNDATION DOCUMENTARY

Lights, Camera . . . Swanton!

SWANTON is about to become the star of a documentary project by **THE ORTON FAMILY FOUNDATION.** From June 5 through June 15, camera crews will be seen all over town interviewing dozens of local residents about the historic forces that shaped Swanton's past, Swanton's current issues and challenges, and the vision that residents have for Swanton's future.

"The 30-minute video will tell the story of Swanton entirely from the point of view of town residents," said film maker Cabot Orton. Orton and Burlington film maker Keith Speigel, both of Slamdunk Productions, will produce and direct the video for The Orton Family Foundation and the Swanton community.

Orton and Spiegel begin shooting background footage for the Swanton video on June 5 and begin interviewing Swanton residents June 8. "We've identified 80 people from all walks of life we will try to interview," said Swanton resident Ron Kilburn. "We keep trying to pare the list back, but then it keeps growing."

Kilburn is president of the Swanton Historical Society and was instrumental in bringing the film crew to Swanton. The Swanton Town and Village Downtown Vitality Task Force designated Kilburn to chair a steering committee that has guided Swanton's involvement in the video.

Kilburn and Bob Hopkins from Missisquoi Valley Union High School, along with a team of Missisquoi Valley students, will conduct additional video interviews to capture archival footage for the Historical Society and maximize the number of residents who can be interviewed for the video. Jenna Speer of Swanton will work as production coordinator with Orton and Spiegel. Residents who have access to old photographs, home movies, or other archival material are encouraged to contact Ron Kilburn.

The final 30-minute broadcast-quality video will be edited and available for a community screening and telecast by early fall.

games, band rehearsals, and school classes are all worth taping. When possible, try to capture annual events like parades, carnivals, or major concerts.

Scouting Locations and Preparing B-roll

It's important to keep in mind that no matter how many different beautiful backdrops you can squeeze out of an interview headquarters location, the background will eventually begin to look repetitive on camera. To avoid this, the production coordinator should arrange several alternate interview locations to use throughout production. This will lend greater visual variety to the finished video and give the owners of your main interview location a well-deserved series of breaks.

B-roll is any footage other than interview footage that is visually cut away to, specifically included throughout a finished video to visually explain or augment what is being said on camera.

Avoid using the same background for interviews. Move around the community. It can also be more relaxing for interview subjects to have the interview done in surroundings familiar to them.

The producers/videographers should also take a long drive around the community during the week before the shoot to seek out and plan "cut-away" shots, also referred to as "B-roll." B-roll is any footage other than interview footage that is visually cut away to, specifically included throughout a finished video to visually explain or augment what is being said on camera. The production manager should make a checklist of all crucial B-roll footage including shots of:

- major buildings and landmarks;
- prominent businesses and public organizations;
- local wilderness areas and public parks;
- people who live in the community; and
- driving shots from a car and aerial or overview (from a high place) shots of the entire community.

The production coordinator can use the B-roll checklist together with the interview schedule to help schedule the production as a whole.

A sheet from the Swanton, Vermont, shooting schedule (with notes). You know that it won't go the way you typed it up. Be flexible and be ready.

By now, the shooting schedule should be mostly complete. The interviews are all set up. Local events to be taped have been determined. B-roll has been planned out. An organization with an historical photo archive has granted permission to put its artifacts on tape. All that remains is for the production coordinator to print copies of the schedule for all the crew members. In other words, it's on to production!

BRANDON, VERMONT, VIDEO SHOOTING SCHEDULE

TUESDAY, JUNE 15TH

9:00 A.M.
FRANK FARNSWORTH
Editor, *The Brandon Bugle*
Location: CVP HEADQUARTERS
(Brandon Inn)

10:00 A.M.
MICHAEL SHANE
Owner, The Lilac Inn
Location: CVP HEADQUARTERS
(Brandon Inn)

11:00 A.M.
MICHAEL BALCH
Brandon Town Manager
Location: CVP HEADQUARTERS
(Brandon Inn)

12:00 Noon
PETER MELLO AND STUDENTS
Principal, The Neshobe School
Location: NESHOBE ELEMENTARYSCHOOL
Route 73 East

1:00 P.M.
LUNCH

2:00 P.M.
DAVE GIBSON
Brandon Selectboard Member
Location: CVP HEADQUARTERS
(Brandon Inn)

3:00 P.M.
Little League Game
Hornets vs. The Builders
Estabrook Field (One mile north of downtown across from the old Brandon Training School)

4:00 P.M.
LYNN SAUNDERS
Brandon Selectboard Chairwoman
Location: CVP HEADQUARTERS (Brandon Inn)
Call to confirm.

5:00 P.M.
ELIZABETH KARNES
Brandon Village Partnership
Location: CVP HEADQUARTERS (Brandon Inn)

6:00 P.M.
DINNER

7:00 P.M.
B-ROLL
Local Farms, the Brandon Training School, the Town Hall and the church steeple, waterfalls, fields, and streams.

8:00 P.M.
B-ROLL
Bingo Game
American Legion

8:45 P.M.
B-ROLL
Sunset from edge of town

PART 3

Production: You're Ready to Go!

It's your first morning. You have all your equipment at the base of operations. The crew arrives. What's the first thing you should do? Get coffee and doughnuts. Well, have an orientation meeting but make sure there are coffee and doughnuts. Make sure each crew member understands his or her role, and that every member of the crew knows what other members will be doing. Review the schedule and invite questions. Many of your crew members might be new to video. Assure them the stupid question is the one that never gets asked.

In the back of your mind, remember: *every* production has its own minor and major crises. The best producers are those who can remain calm when problems arise. This will, in turn, inspire peace of mind and confidence in the crew. The first rule in being a producer is very simple: Don't panic!

When the first interview subject arrives, the production manager should inform the interviewee that the first set-up of the shoot always takes a little longer and that he or she may have to wait 15 minutes before the taping begins. This will prepare the person for potential delays so that he or she won't get impatient.

DOCUMENTARY RELEASE FORM

If your Video Project is intended for repeated public broadcast, including local cable stations, it's a good idea to secure permission from each participant to use his or her appearance in the video. (A sample form from the Fruita, Colorado, Community Video Project appears on the following page.) During the wait, have the interviewee sign a documentary "release form" legally granting the producers the right to use the person's image and likeness in a video production. An easy release form that's not too wordy or intimidating can be designed like a petition, with the release conditions at the top of the page and people's signatures following underneath. Remember that interviewees under the age of 18 need their parents or guardians to sign for them.

FRUITA, COLORADO, COMMUNITY VIDEO RELEASE FORM

I hereby grant the City of Fruita and The Orton Family Foundation permission to use my image and likeness for the Fruita Community Video Project and its future public broadcast in all forms.

Print Name   Date

Signature   Phone Number

E-mail Address

BASICS OF THE VIDEO SHOOT
Camera Set-Up

The first steps of setting up are basic: securing the camcorder onto the tripod and assembling the lights. Once the camcorder is turned on, there are five basic steps that are always necessary before an interview can begin:

1. Lighting the shot
2. Setting the camcorder's "white balance"
3. Getting the "critical focus" of the shot
4. Framing the shot
5. "Miking" the interview subject

Each of these steps is outlined in detail below.

Lighting the shot. There is almost nothing more important than proper lighting. It's easy to light your shots properly, and learning how to use a lighting kit or the sun is a fundamental step to becoming a skilled videographer.

First, let's consider how to use a lighting kit. "Three-point lighting" is a basic setup for interviews that you can master with any pro lighting kit or with three halogen shop lights. The three points in the setup are: (1) key light; (2) fill light; and (3) back light. The three lights are arranged in a circle around your interview subject, who sits in the center, looking at the camera or at you, the interviewer, sitting next to the camera. The three lights and camera are like points on a clock: key light at 4:30, camera at 6:00, fill light at 8:00, back light at 11:00.

The key light, as the name implies, is the main light in the setup. It goes right next to the camera or just a few feet to its side. (If you're standing behind the camera, the key light goes on the right side.) The key light sits on its stand and points down at the subject's head at an angle of around 35 degrees. Adjust the key light so it doesn't shine directly into the subject's eyes. Start with the key light next to the camera and you will see it creates flat light with no shadows around the subject.

The fill light is a larger, softer light and serves to fill shadows created by the key light. It sits on the circle at 8:00 (on the left side of the camera if you're standing behind it). It should be slightly lower than the camera, pointing down at the subject at an angle of 25 degrees. The fill light can be used to create a warm mood for your subject. Experiment with the tone it creates by moving it side to side and by changing the angle at which it falls on the subject. Watch the monitor to see what works for the setup.

The camera operator setting up on site. Consult the text for the five basic set-up steps before any interview can begin.

The back light is similar to the key light and sits behind the subject, higher than the other two lights. It's used to create a three-dimensional feeling in the lighting setup and will make the subject stand out from the background. Put it at 11:00 on the circle and experiment with it to create different silhouettes and halos. Watch the monitor closely; if your subject's halo is too intense, point the back light more toward the background instead of directly at the subject. Be sure to avoid getting the back light in the shot. Also, don't point it directly at the camera unless you want to overload the exposure.

It may take a little while to achieve an ideal setup when you first start learning how to use lights. Your interview subject may get bored, impatient, or restless, especially in a stuffy room with hot lights glaring (temporarily) in the person's face. To ease this tension, have someone else in the room exclaim that the shot is amazing and definitely worth the effort.

Lighting with the sun presents different challenges and opportunities. If you know how to adapt to its whims, the sun can work to your advantage as a lighting source, often creating unusual opportunities.

It's usually best to avoid direct sunlight on indoor shoots; windows can sometimes throw a harsh light on your subject that looks natural to the eye but creates too much contrast for a camera. This is because your camera has nowhere near the range of adjustment and sensitivity as the human eye. If you can't move your indoor shot away from a window, try pulling blinds, a shade, or putting a blanket over the window to diffuse the light and use the three-point system to create a good lighting setup.

Everything changes when you take your camera outside. You have an endless source of natural light that can be used in extremely effective ways. Often, we find that interviews outdoors, with nature as its own beautiful backdrop, look better than indoors. Sometimes, however, sunlight is too flat and harsh, particularly between 10 A.M. and 3 P.M. on sunny days. You will find that shady places are your best bet to shoot outdoor interviews on sunny days, as they can transform hard sunlight into diffuse, ambient light on the subject, while the background behind the subject is out in the sun and brightly, beautifully lit. Shaded setups are a great way to go if you're going to shoot interviews outside. Pull out the reflector boards and let the camera roll.

Using a reflector board . . .

If the sun is really bright during a particular indoor shoot, and you think you can get away without using your lighting kit, pull out the white foam board or auto sun reflector you bought. These will reflect natural light to fill in shadows around your subject. Usually, a reflector board can be put on the floor at the subject's feet (out of the camera frame) and angled up towards the subject's face. Reflector boards can also be attached to light stands with clothes pins, duct tape, or whatever comes handy. If you're going with natural light indoors, you can also try hanging plain old white bed sheets over the windows to soften the light coming in. Don't be afraid to try different combinations and techniques.

(Left) Setting up the lights. (Right) Note the position of the three lights. Imagine a clock face with the interview subject at 12:00. The key light is at 4:30; the camera is at 6:00; the fill light is at 8:00; and the back light is at 11:00.

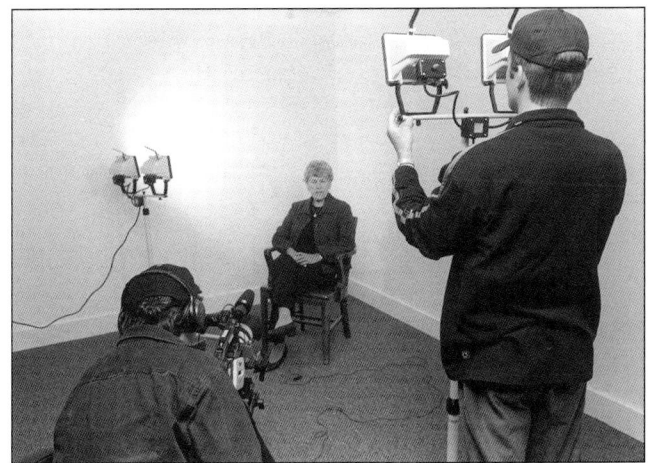
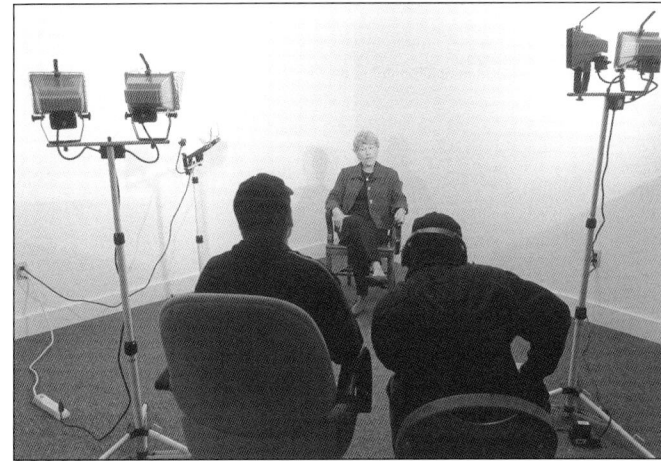

Working with the sun...
If you're getting set up to interview outside, don't have your subject face into the sun. Sunlight is many times brighter than a halogen lamp, and your subject will tend to peer and squint in a highly unflattering manner throughout the interview. Rather than have subjects wear sunglasses, seat them in the shade and use reflector boards to direct sunlight where it needs to go.

A very nice halo effect can sometimes be achieved by having a subject sit with low sun directly at their back. Also, the setting sun casts a wonderful red-amber glow on people's faces and can make anyone look like Lawrence of Arabia gazing heroically across the desert.

You've probably heard that Hollywood directors call the time outdoors during sunrise and sunset the "Magic Hour." There's a good reason for this. Sunlight takes on dramatic, almost emotional qualities at dawn and at dusk, and does for landscapes what it does for interview subjects: it romanticizes them with light. We always make a point of leaving our schedule open during these times of the day in order to capture as much location footage as possible. Even with the tightest scheduling, there never seems to be enough time to shoot when the sun starts to cast its special glow on a town. Everything in those short minutes takes on a new life for the camera: buildings, trees, faces, even cars. Some of the best shots we've ever taken have emerged from frantic sprints with a camera during sunset.

Setting the white balance. Once you've finished lighting the shot, the next step is to set a function on your camcorder called the "white balance." This function enables the camcorder to accurately record all the colors of the spectrum in an image by setting them relative to pure white.

Amazingly, the color white changes with every lighting situation. The sun provides a very different "color temperature" than an incandescent bulb indoors. These differences in color temperature will create drastically different tints on camera; the only way to correct for these differences is to set the white balance.

To set the white balance, zoom in on a completely white surface such as a sheet of paper or the back of a white T-shirt. Then hit the camcorder's "set white balance" button. A graphic in the viewfinder will begin flashing for a few seconds, and when it's done the white balance has been set.

Once the white balance has been configured, the lighting setup should not be changed in any way. If there are any such changes, the white balance will have to be reset again.

Getting the critical focus. With the interview subject in place, the shot now needs to be focused. If the focus is set with the shot framed wide, there is very little flexibility for adjusting the zoom range of the shot during the interview. The moment the camcorder starts zooming in or out, the shot will start to go blurry. The way to correct for this problem before taping begins is to perform a technique called "critical focus."

The white balance function on a camcorder (top) adjusts the camera's ability to record colors by setting them relative to white. To set the white balance, the camera operator needs to focus on a solid white object. Here, it's a solid white board (bottom).

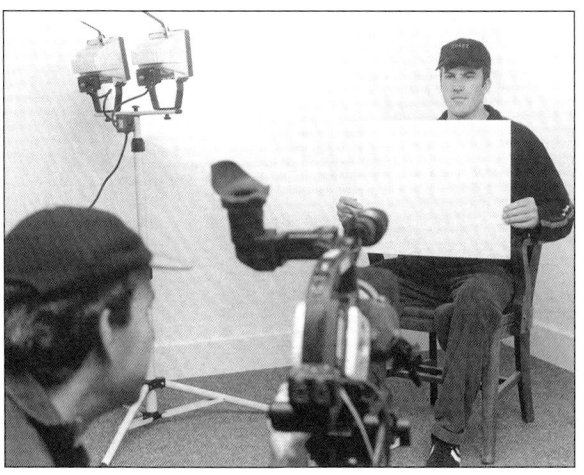

To achieve the critical focus, just zoom in on your subject as far as the camcorder will go. The shot will probably now be of the person's nostril. Then adjust the focus ring so that this extreme close-up is perfectly in focus. When you zoom out of this shot, you'll notice that every point from the closest zoom to the widest shot is completely in focus, allowing the camera operator to zoom in on a person at any point in an interview.

Using the camera lens to achieve "critical focus"—the technique that allows you to move from close zoom to wide shot without having to refocus—is essential to any shot.

Framing the shot. There are a few basic guidelines for creating professional-looking shot composition. Start by adjusting the tripod's height slightly lower than the subject's eye-line. In general, keep the shot tight. This will emphasize the person rather than the background and make it easier for the viewer to focus on what the person is saying. Make sure there's not too much "head room," the distance between the top of the person's head and the top of the visual frame. Fill the extra part of the frame with a backdrop that aesthetically complements the person's face in terms of symmetry, color, and shadows. Avoid backgrounds such as wild patterns (wallpaper), overly bright backgrounds (a white building in the sun), mirrors, or anything that will distract from the person giving the interview.

The composition of the image in the frame means taking into consideration objects in the background (note the American flag on the left) that complement the main subject—in this case, an elderly gentleman reflecting on his community's past.

 **PART 3 HIGHLIGHTS:**
Production: We're ready to go! . . .

• Make sure the people you interviewed sign a release form

• The basics of a shooting interview include:
  1. lighting the shot;
  2. setting the camcorder's white balance;
  3. getting the "critical focus" of the shot;
  4. framing the shot; and
  5. "miking" the interview subject.

• Timecode helps you keep track of your video footage. To keep accurate timecode, make sure that the camcorder is paused at the very end of your previous footage before you start taping again.

• The first question of any interview should never be controversial or complex. Begin with a simple question that the subject can answer easily. As an interview progresses, the main challenge facing an interviewer is to encourage the subject to deliver articulate, well-formulated, "punchy" statements.

• The best time of day to shoot outdoor B-roll footage is when the sun is going down.

• Historical photographs can be videotaped directly from a photograph or scanned into a JPEG file and manipulated with editing software.

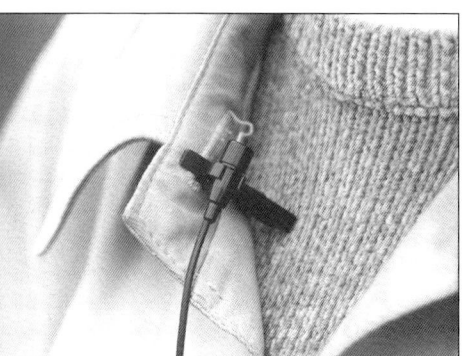 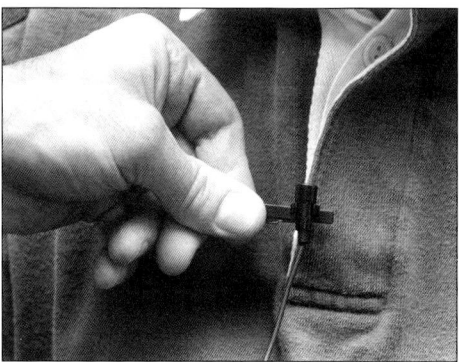 

The Lavolier microphone (left) is small enough that it will not be obtrusive in the shot. It simply clips on an individual's lapel (middle). When attaching the lav, work with the interview subject to hide the cable up a sleeve or under a collar (right).

Miking the shot. Now that the video portion is set up, the last thing that remains is sound. As we discussed in the Equipment section above, in the equipment section, the standard microphone used for conducting documentary interviews is the tiny Lavolier microphone (the lav).

The basic lav consists of a raisin-sized microphone, connected by a long cord to a big XLR plug that contains a double-A battery and has an on/off switch. The lav should also come with a little foam screen that shields the mike from wind noise. The XLR "male" plug end of the lav goes into an adapter on your camera, and the microphone clips onto your subject's lapel, shirt pocket, or tie. The mike should be placed near enough to the subject's chest to pick up vocal resonance.

When attaching the lav to the interview subject, the best place to run the cable is up through a shirt, jacket, or coat so that it is hidden from view. You'll need to politely ask your interview subject to snake the cable up for you. If it doesn't work to have the interviewee run the mike wire through a sleeve, throw the cable over a shoulder and tuck it in around the collar. Another option is simply to keep the shot very tight on the person's head, thus eliminating the cable in the visual frame.

It takes a little time to position the lav for optimal audio. Place the mike between 7 and 10 inches below your subject's chin. If you bury it too far underneath the chin, your audio sound is going to be muffled. If it is too low, you'll pick up distracting noises. Don't forget about the lav once it's clipped in place. Keep checking to make sure that the mike is pointing directly toward your interviewee's mouth. You should reposition or remove necklaces and other jewelry or clothing that may come into contact with the lav.

If you're shooting outdoors, you probably want to use a "windscreen," a dark fuzzy cover that comes with all lavs. Though using a windscreen will make it harder to hide the mike, you will find that it works better than anything else to filter out unwanted noise. Be sure to put the windscreen back in its case along with the microphone kit when it is not in use. This will prevent loss and difficulty finding it when you need it.

Wireless lavs are very convenient if you want to do an interview without having your subject tethered to the camera, as with a walking interview. Unfortunately, sometimes the cable between the clip-on mike and the wireless transmitter can act like an antenna, picking up interference and unwanted radio signals, so don't wrap extra cable into a ball or loop when you're setting up the wireless lav.

Always wear headphones! There are many things that can go wrong with your lav during a shoot: the external mike cord can come unplugged from the camera, a microphone battery can wear out, the lav may brush

Keep an eye on that microphone and battery . . .

Always remember to turn on both the transmitter unit and the receiving units of the wireless. Otherwise you'll have complete silence on your interview.

Wireless lavs are also notorious for running their batteries out. Change your batteries regularly and carry plenty of spares, as you will feel especially foolish if you lose the lav during an interview and are forced to use the camera's built-in mike. Worse, you may not notice that the lav has died and you're recording silence.

up against the interviewee's clothes, or a plane may fly overhead just as you're getting to the point of the interview. The only way to prevent these situations from ruining your footage is to constantly monitor your audio by listening with a set of headphones.

Almost all camcorders have a "headphone jack" output on the side. A few cameras also have a device called a "VU Meter," which allows you to read the audio levels with a bouncing needle or digital display as you record. These meters are great for making sure that your audio doesn't "peak out" and become distorted.

Preserving Control Track on Mini-DV Tapes

Digital camcorders will automatically encode every single frame of tape that you shoot with its own special number called "timecode." (More on this below in the Editing section.) This timecode will be necessary for identifying the clips later on.

Here's one thing we must emphasize strongly: if you are using a DV camcorder, *don't stop and replay the DV tape before the entire tape has been used.* Many of us have a tendency to shoot interviews or other footage and then rewind the tape to check what we've just shot. *Doing this will screw up your timecode!* This is because the camcorder will start the timecode over at zero each time you stop and replay a tape. The result will be "holes" in the tape's control track. This will make it extremely difficult to find clips later on during the digitizing process because all the clips on each tape will be identified in your editing script only by their corresponding timecodes.

To put it in simple terms, *make sure that the camcorder is paused at the very end of your previous footage before you start taping again.*

Labeling Tapes

It may sound inconsequential, but properly labeling your videotapes is absolutely crucial for keeping the footage in order. The camera operator or production coordinator (whoever has the neatest handwriting) should be responsible for accurately numbering and labeling the side and front of each tape, and then safely storing each tape in a small box or case. If possible, write the contents of each tape on the big part of its label (interviews, B-roll shots, etc.).

We suggest using separate tapes for interviews, B-roll, and history footage. This will make your life considerably easier when you begin logging and digitizing your footage.

The camera operator needs a good set of headphones and needs to keep them on to make sure that he or she knows what the lav microphone is exactly picking up (and what it isn't). This will guard against the worst-case scenario—the lav becoming unplugged from the camera without the camera operator noticing.

Mini-DV tapes are quite different from the bulky VHS tapes that were in vogue 10 years ago.

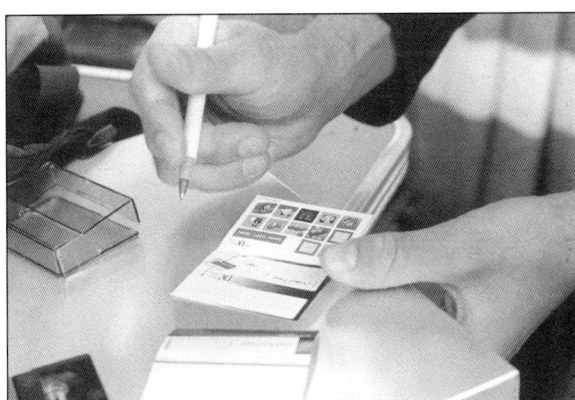

It's always the little things that throw us. And regarding Community Video Projects, one of the essential little things is labeling tapes to make sure you keep your footage in order.

SAMPLE INTERVIEW DIALOGUE

Morristown, Vermont

INTERVIEWER: You mentioned the downtown. What positive changes have you noticed in that part of town over the past five years?

WHITNEY KAULBACH: I think over the past four to five years living in the area we've seen the downtown go from being almost desolate to becoming a real downtown again. We saw a bakery go in, a coffee shop, the gravel bike path at the end of Main Street, and projects that the kids have done—such as painting garbage cans—so you can see the revival of the town. The reason the town became so desolate is you see the Price Chopper and Grand Union out on what's almost a strip so there's already been that struggle there. I think that it would be devastating to lose the downtown. Having the downtown is what keeps our community together.

Brandon, Vermont

INTERVIEWER: What can local government do to deal with an issue such as continuing increase in heavy traffic?

EDWARD BARNA: Change has to take place at the highest level of government. They have to admit that people are not going to leave the motorcar behind, that trucks will always be used for business and we are going to need traffic bypasses—and if it's going take a long time and cost a lot, then that's all the more reason to start NOW, and spread the cost out over time. It's not an excuse to say "we're not gonna do anything."

THE ART OF THE INTERVIEW

The technical issues have been resolved for the moment, and everyone is feeling a sense of relief. But the most exquisitely lit shot in the world is not going to be much good if the person being interviewed is a nervous wreck.

Prior to interviews, interviewers should have at their sides a basic list of potential questions suited to the particular person being interviewed. The interviewer should know some information about the person being interviewed. This information can be used to formulate questions about those aspects of the community with which the interviewee is most knowledgeable.

Sitting in front of a camera under glaring hot lights is enough to make almost anyone feel jittery. The video interviewer (who in many cases will also be the camera operator) should make a point of informally chatting with the person before the camera is ever turned on. The interviewee should be offered a glass of water and provided with a comfortable chair. The first question of any interview should never be controversial or complex; on the contrary, interviews should always begin with a simple question that the subject can answer easily, such as what the person does for work or enjoyment.

As an interview progresses, the main challenge facing an interviewer is to encourage the subject to deliver articulate, well-formulated, "punchy" statements. Some interview subjects are already well schooled for performing on camera and will automatically package their verbal statements into nice, neat (but not too nice and neat) sound bites. This type of interview subject is a rare but potentially valuable source of quotes.

For less media-savvy people, there are some techniques the interviewer can use to encourage thoughtful answers. The most important ground rule is to prevent people from giving standard, memorized responses that sound like they're being read from a page. Questions should be phrased in a way that elicits spontaneous or emotional reactions, without inviting vague or generic replies.

Finally, there are some interview subjects who will drone on regardless of how far off the main subject they've gotten. When this type of interviewee is being taped, the polite way to end the interview quickly is to ask a final summarizing question such as, What, in conclusion, do you see as your town's single greatest strength? Then thank him or her for participating and shut off the camera.

The final questions posed should be the most broad reaching and provocative, regardless of the quality of the interview as a whole. Common questions we have used at the end of interviews include:

- How do you see your town changing in 5 or 10 years?
- If you could change one thing about your town in the near future, what would that be?
- Summarize the character of your town in a single word or phrase....
- What has living in this community meant to you as a person?

SHOOTING THE VIDEO
Shooting B-roll

The technical guidelines for taping B-roll footage are at first identical to taping sit-down interviews:

1. Set the white balance (in this case, usually to "sunlight")
2. Get the critical focus
3. Frame the shot

"B-roll" shots can be used throughout your video to add variety. If you can get some interesting perspectives (like, from a crane or helicopter), great. But just shooting through the open window of a car may give you what you want.

The main difference between B-roll and interview footage is that with B-roll, the camera is often (but not always) outside and hand-held instead of on a tripod.

The main difference between B-roll and interview footage is that with B-roll, the camera is often (but not always) outside and hand-held instead of on a tripod.

Hand-held shots will create visual variety in your piece and can add energy and drama as cutaways to illustrate interviews. Swish pans from one object to another, quick zoom-outs and zoom-ins, and "rack focus" shots (which involve shifting the focus from a foreground object to a background object or vice-versa) are all commonly used techniques. Shooting out of the open window of a moving vehicle is another way to bring energy to a video.

Some B-roll shots may still be taken with a tripod. This is especially appropriate for establishing formal shots of a location or building and for tranquil shots of people in repose or landscapes that are not meant to suggest action. Again, the best time of day to shoot outdoor B-roll footage is when the sun is going down. Try to plan as much of the B-roll footage shooting as possible around this time. You won't regret it.

Ideas for additional B-roll footage will evolve throughout the production process. During interviews, people will inevitably begin touching on identical points. A production assistant should take note of these common references throughout the shoot, so that corresponding B-roll cutaways can be filmed to specifically match these statements.

Shooting Historical Materials

Capturing historical artifacts on tape can be a time-consuming but rewarding process. For history buffs, there's nothing more exciting than taking an old photograph and making it come to life in great detail on screen.

Whether you're taping your photographs at a local historical society or in someone's basement, the process is essentially the same: mount the photographs onto a flat surface, set your camcorder on its tripod, and start taping. An item we have found to be effective for mounting photographs is an easel. We hold the photographs in place with clothes pins,

Some historical materials will need to be removed from frames and provided with a good background to show well on the video. Using the tripod and an easel can create a good, steady shot of an important document or map.

which won't cause any damage. If there's no easel handy, a bulletin board will do. Just attach a piece of paper to the board and paperclip each photograph to the sides of the paper to keep it in place.

If you're in a hurry, you can even place a photograph or map on the floor and point the camcorder downward. However, this method is not recommended, as it does not allow the camera operator to do any sort of horizontal pan shots.

Photographs should not be lit with direct light, as this can create major glare from a photo's shiny surface. Bounce the light off the ceiling or a bounce board. It's surprising how little light can be sufficient for a tiny photograph.

Don't let all your historical photographs be dull static shots, in which the camera doesn't move. Old photos can be brought to life by tilting the camera up or down, panning left to right across a shot, and zooming in or out of a point on the shot. The powerful zooms of digital video camcorders can be used to show a small part of a photograph in fine detail, then the camera can simultaneously pan across and zoom out to smoothly reveal the rest of the shot.

One effective device in videotaping photographs is to reveal information about the shot with a tilt, pan, or zoom. An example of this technique might be to start with a late-1800s photograph of some citizens standing outside a building, and then tilting the camera up to reveal a sign above their heads reading: "HOTEL GRAND OPENING."

A new and better option for recording historical photos is to simply scan the photos into a JPEG file, using a flatbed scanner and a computer. The digital file can then be loaded directly into a nonlinear editing system, and special effects programs such as *Adobe After Effects* can be used to manipulate the photos, creating amazing pans, zooms, and other visual motion. This is how virtually all television documentaries process images today. If you have access to a computer, scanner and editing effects software, we very enthusiastically recommend using this method.

Finally, be sure not to limit the video's historical images to photographs. As we mentioned in the history checklist, there are a variety of artifacts that can be used to establish history, such as maps, letters, the town charter, paintings, newspaper headlines, and even local business advertisements.

Well, you have everything recorded. Now what do you do? In one word: edit. And Part 4 will teach you how.

Here, a historical photo is placed on the floor, and the camera operator zooms in or pans across the photo to create an effect.

PART 4

Post-production: After the Shoot

Now that your Community Video is completely shot and you've had a couple days to recuperate from the shoot, we have some good news and some bad news. The bad news is that the real work has just begun. You're not even close to being finished yet. But the good news is that you're now entering the most creative and enriching phase of your project: editing.

In a nutshell, editing is the process of whittling down your hours of raw footage into a coherent, "viewer-friendly" piece. This is accomplished by reviewing all your tapes in order to identify the most desirable footage.

Once you single out the moments of the raw footage that you want to use, you can arrange these clips in an order that flows together to make the video work as a whole. During the process, you can add in sounds that weren't recorded onto your original raw footage, such as narration and music. There are no limits to the possibilities of how your footage can be put together. This can be both mind numbing and exhilarating at the same time. Surgeon General's Warning: Editing is addictive.

Before you go into the editing room, you have to know all your footage backwards and forwards. You need to be able to carefully review almost every moment that you shot, marking down exactly where each scene occurs on a specific tape. That way, when you arrive in the editing room you won't have to spend hours shuffling through footage. This process of reviewing raw footage and making notes on its contents is called "logging." It's painfully tedious, but you'll be prepared when you get into the editing room.

With tapes in hand (literally), you can begin your editing process. The first step is logging. While tedious, it's absolutely necessary and will get you very well acquainted with your footage.

Logging your footage directly from the camcorder . . .

If you own the camcorder with which you shot your Community Video and there are no time constraints for using it, you can get away with logging your footage directly from the camcorder (or from a monitor to which it's hooked up). You have to be able to read the timecode either from the camcorder's viewfinder or from a digital display on its side. Most DV camcorders have this capability; some can even display timecode when you hook them up to a monitor. Since this puts extra wear and tear on your camcorder's playback heads and on the source tapes, this method of logging is not recommended. If you do use this method, be certain to buy and use a video head-cleaning tape for your camcorder.

In order to start logging, you must first have copies of your raw footage capable of repeated viewing without wearing down the original source tape or your camcorder. The best way to do this is to make copies ("dubs") of all your footage on ordinary VHS tapes. The quality of these tapes is not very important; they are used for editing purposes.

Once you've finished dubbing all your footage onto VHS, you need to find a VCR that can read and display SMTPE (real time) timecode. This is a numeric system that assigns each video frame a number based on a 24-hour clock. It allows editors to pinpoint a frame, enabling precise edits. For instance, if an interview begins at exactly 5 minutes and 30 seconds into your raw footage, the timecode would read 00:05:30.

Not all VCRs have the capability to display timecode on the screen. Most older models display a more primitive device called a "counter." The "counter code" only consists of a four-digit number that moves along with your footage, but that doesn't accurately reflect passing hours, minutes, and seconds. It is extremely important to remember that counter code is *not* adequate for logging purposes! Counter code does not increase at regular intervals; the time on your tape between 0-100 may be five minutes while the time between 100-200 may be eight minutes. There's simply no way to tell.

So when you find a VCR that displays SMPTE timecode, you're ready to start logging. The easiest way to type in your footage log is with a laptop computer, but any computer will work. Make sure you have a remote control handy for the VCR because you're probably going to be stopping and starting it every couple of minutes. When you pop in your first videotape, rewind it to the very beginning and be sure to hit "reset" on the VCR's remote. This way the timecode on the beginning of the tape will be set to 00:00:00.

Now start watching your footage. When you come to a point on the tape that strikes you as significant or memorable, hit "pause." Type in the timecode of that point, followed by a quick notation and key word reminding you of the shot. If someone makes a grand or articulate statement, type it in. If you see a majestic or panoramic shot, mark it down. The more detailed you are in the log, the better. It will make your life easier when you sit down to write your editing script.

WRITING THE EDITING SCRIPT
Identifying Key Topics

Now that you're finished with your log, you've earned the right to take a step back for a moment and start to think about your video project as a whole. In the long process of logging, you no doubt became intimately familiar with your footage. Glance at your log and you'll see that people probably kept bringing up recurring or key topics. Type the various topic headings or key words, which can be narrowed down, into a new word processing file on your computer and you've just begun the process of creating your editing script, which is entirely driven by the information you collected from your community members.

Arranging Interview Clips

The next step is to group together all pertinent interview clips related to each topic. For the moment, these clips do not need to go in any particular order; just try to group each topic's clips together. The quickest way to pick out all the great quotes in your log is to use the computer's "find" function and type in a keyword. For example, if one of your topics is the traffic downtown, just do a "find" in your log document for the word "traffic."

Once you reach a quote that you want to use, highlight the entire quote and its corresponding timecode number in your log document and hit "copy." Then go back to your editing script document and go to the particular clip's topic heading. "Paste" it underneath the topic. Continue collecting the rest of the clips about the topic, until you reach the end of the log. Then move on to the next topic. If you've logged your footage thoroughly, you should have no problem finding plenty of good thoughtful statements with this method. When you've finished filling in all the topics with a variety of clips, it's time to start creating a coherent narrative out of the random assortment of topics you now have in front of you.

Think about your Community Video as a whole for a moment. On what kind of note do you want the piece to begin? How do you want to introduce the topics? How do you want to explore issues? On what kind of note do you want to leave your viewers?

These questions are crucial for creating a video that can powerfully convey meaning to its audience. To hold the viewer's attention, it helps to create logical and smooth transitions between featured topics. The first step toward accomplishing this is to group together closely related topics. This is a subjective process, but it shouldn't be difficult to find common denominators. For a rudimentary example, consider the following. Let's say five of your topic headings include:

- threat of sprawl;
- downtown traffic problem;
- the proposed bypass;
- lack of cultural events in town; and
- need for downtown revitalization.

What you will find is that many of your issues are connected. The reason why your city council is proposing a bypass in the first place is because of the traffic problem, right? So put traffic first, then the bypass issue. Now look at some of the interview clips you have under "bypass." Some people are worried that a bypass may draw potential business away from downtown, thus creating "sprawl." Sprawl, then, is placed after bypass.

Now you probably have two topics left. Look over the reasons why people are calling for downtown revitalization. Perhaps people have expressed anxiety that their community could become a ghost town if the traffic gets routed around it with a bypass. Some people probably propose that to avoid this problem, the downtown must be revitalized and made into a fun place to spend time. There is a nice transition from the problem of "sprawl" to the solution of "downtown revitalization."

The last topic, lack of cultural events in town, is really a subcategory of downtown revitalization. After all, a thriving downtown tends to already have theater, galleries, eateries, and music. If the downtown is in dire need of economic repair, the chances are it won't have lots of Shakespeare-In-The-Park-type events paid for by the town. You can include "lack of cultural events" under downtown revitalization, and you've got a smooth-flowing script.

Now that you've got topic headings in order, you can start rearranging the clips within each category to help create even smoother transitions between topics. For example, if you're trying to segue from the "proposed bypass" issue to the accompanying "threat of sprawl" issue, you might want to end the bypass section with an interview clip about the various downsides of the bypass. This would nicely set up the topic of "sprawl." You could then begin the "sprawl" section with a comment from someone

✓ **EDITING CHECKLIST**

Editing can be an extremely rewarding process if you take the time to:

❏ line up an editor in advance who will help arrange for a system;

❏ arrange for an editing system, preferably nonlinear, that works for your budget;

❏ log all of your footage thoroughly;

❏ write a detailed editing script, including a historical timeline, narration, and montages;

❏ maintain a clear idea of the style, tone, and pace you want to convey in the video; and

❏ work with the steering committee to ensure balance, accuracy, and appeal

If you've logged your footage thoroughly, you should have no problem finding plenty of good thoughtful statements. . . .

SAMPLE EDITING SCRIPT: SWANTON, VERMONT

NARRATOR, Swanton Downtown: During the 1970s Swanton struggled to rebound from a devastating fire, rebuilding its business district in a modern style. The 1970 fire was not the last blaze to consume a historic part of Swanton. In 1987, the covered railway bridge over the Missisquoi River—the longest of its kind in the country—burned before dawn.

TAPE 4, 25:20, Neal Speer, long-time resident: I was awoken by the crackling and the glow outside of my bedroom window. I went down across the street and looked down the river just in time to see the whole framework of the bridge falling into the river. It was a real eerie sight. Everything was a ball of fire and it dropped right into the river, so part of Swanton's history went right in the river. It was a sad day.

NARRATOR, Abenaki Revival: The 1970s saw the revival of the Missisquoi Abenaki community, a people who had been in hiding for many years. In the early 1990s the Abenaki began their annual heritage celebration, which moved to the Swanton village green in May of 2000.

NARRATOR, Swanton History to Current Day: To this day Swanton retains close ties to its past. A number of its historic buildings have been restored for present day use, including the Robin Hood ammunition factory-—now an industrial complex-—and the former Swanton high school, currently being renovated as housing for senior citizens. Recently, a group of citizens led by the Swanton Historical Society banded together to save the historic railway depot building—the last standing railway structure in town. The entire building was relocated across from the former sight of the covered railroad bridge.

TAPE 7, 30:04, Ron Kilburn, President, Swanton Historical Society: On a day that was one day before our deadline, we were able to pick up that building, put it on the train, move it down the tracks, and get it to this location where we are hopefully going to restore it.

TAPE 2, 12:21, Roger Livingston, Swanton Chamber of Commerce: I was amazed! I did go down that day and they jacked and jacked and jacked and jacked . . . until they got it to a certain point and then put it on a couple of flat beds and pulled it with an engine about a quarter of a mile. It was quite an operation, no damage.

TAPE 2, 47:37, Evan Speer, Student: It was really cool to see a whole building . . . that was like 500 feet long . . . in the air and on a railroad bed. I was like "Whoa."

NARRATOR, Modern Swanton: Today, Swanton remains a diverse close-knit community that maintains strong ties to neighboring cities both north and south of the Canadian border. Nestled between rich farmland and an expansive wilderness area, Swanton has managed to retain the distinct rural character while facing new challenges for the twenty-first century.

NARRATOR, Canada: Swanton's proximity to Canada gives the town an international flair with strong cultural and economic influences from Quebec.

TAPE 5, 10:35, Leon Berhiaum, CEO of St. Albans Co-op Creamery: Being in the northwest corner of Vermont certainly has its advantages. Certainly, being again right on the border to Canada certainly I think has provided for us many tourists. To come to the States, certainly as they come into the States obviously one of the first communities they come across is our community.

TAPE 4, 5:12, Ed Daniel, Educator: I think that we have a unique situation, a common background, remember there is nowhere else in the world or in the United States where people have been able to emigrate to the United States and then go home for supper.

about how the symptoms of sprawl include a lack of bustling activity downtown. You can then veer off into the other problems of sprawl and how it endangers the community.

It's important to remember that this is just an example of editing script, and that when you're in the editing room, it will be much easier to see which clips can be juxtaposed, and which clips should be thrown out entirely. It can be hard to determine a person's intonation on a particular comment from the log itself. You will at least have all your relevant clips grouped together and the timecode to tell you how to find them.

Writing Present-Day Narration

Writing narration can do a great deal to lend a personal voice to a video. Good narration can seamlessly connect many seemingly disparate topics. Narration should be filled in under each topic heading. When you write narration, try to take into account all the clips from the topic at hand and come up with a sentence that reflects a balanced perspective on the topic. Be sure to refine this piece of narration so that it contributes to a smooth transition from the previous topic. This can be tricky, but also fun.

Going back to our sample script above, let's try writing narration for the "lack of cultural events" section. This topic comes right after "downtown revitalization," and will need to be tied to it. Let's first glance over the many interview sound bites we have about "lack of cultural events."

Suppose you have taped an angry teenage girl complaining that there are never any cool bands in town on weekends, a theater professor wishing there were more support for local productions, a city commissioner who doesn't want to see local tax dollars spent on museums, and an art council president arguing that a summer theater would draw hundreds of rich tourists into town who would spend money at all the shops. Taking all this into account, the narration for this section might go something like this: "Many residents believe that the downtown currently lacks a broad selection of cultural events."

The order of this section's clips might be the following.

1. The art council president's comment
2. The angry teenage girl and the theater professor to illustrate different forms of the same problem
3. The city commissioner with a dissenting opinion
4. Another clip from the town art council president

When you are arranging the clips, you may find that some topics feature an inordinate number of interview bites. A topic may be too complex to discuss in one section. In this case, it's a good idea to divide the topic into two or three different sections, each with its own piece of narration. Take the issue of "downtown revitalization" from our above example. This issue could encompass restoring damaged buildings, repaving sidewalks, bringing in more locally owned businesses, organizing outdoor concerts in the park, building a recreation center, etc. There's easily enough information here to break up the issue into three sections.

1. Improving the physical appearance of downtown
2. Strengthening downtown businesses
3. Creating more activities downtown

Each of these new sections should have its own narration.

Be sensitive to what is being said and in what manner . . .

You may have a terrific quote from an individual that wonderfully illustrates a point you have heard over and over again as part of your interviews; however, there's one problem. The quote was made light-heartedly, and the person being interviewed may be seriously embarrassed if the quote is immortalized in perpetuity as part of your Community Video. Please be sensitive. You are interviewing real people with real lives in your community, and you could cause them irreparable damage. Sometimes, you'll just have to let that quote go.

A topic may be too complex to discuss in one section. In this case, it's a good idea to divide the topic into two or three different sections, each with its own piece of narration.

PART 4 HIGHLIGHTS:

Post-production: After the shoot . . .

- Editing is the process of whittling down your hours of raw footage into a coherent, "viewer-friendly" piece. Line up an editor in advance who knows the software and understands what you are trying to produce.

- Know your footage frontwards and backwards before going into the editing room. Timecode helps you identify specific places on your video footage.

- To write an editing script:
  1. Identify key topics
  2. Arrange the interview clips that illustrate the topics
  3. Write the narration script to go with the interview clips
  4. Write a historical narration that ties historical events to the present and the future
  5. Piece together montages to illustrate specific themes about the community

- Digital editing systems require reasonably high-speed and high-memory capacity on a computer. Good places to look for such machines are video departments at local schools or at your local cable access television studio.

- Have your steering committee review a first cut of your video before moving on to a final version. Pay special attention to making sure all credits and titles are correct.

- Music can add local flavor to your video. Be sure you have permission to use copyrighted music.

Writing Historical Narration

Once you're finished writing narration for all the topics, there is one major section left: history. Besides giving your video's audience familiar territory to consider at the start, local history provides a frame of reference for modern day issues and events. History helps to create a sense of perspective, to explain why things became the way they are, to show how local choices by ordinary people directly affect the places people inhabit. Rather than create an isolated, self-contained look at a community's past, your job here is to tie history to the present and even the future, and to show that things always have a way of repeating themselves.

The historical events of a community might include the following.

1. Town Charter (1795)
2. First grist mill (1810)
3. Residents who fought in Civil War (1863)
4. Railroad built in town, ushering in Industrial Era (1885)
5. First county fair (1898)
6. Town library built (1910)
7. Automobiles first widely used in town (1925)
8. The Great Depression forces town iron foundry to close down (1933)
9. Boom in tourism after World War II (1950s)
10. New zoning policy initiated (1971)

Which of these events is worth including? It's a matter of opinion, but as a rule of thumb, it's more interesting to focus on events from the most recent century than the distant past. An event such as the Civil War was extremely significant on a national scale, but was it especially important for your town in particular? If not, maybe you could just mention it briefly in the narration without devoting an entire section to it.

On the other hand, suppose one of the major themes in the video is the decline of industry in the town and how industry has been replaced by tourism. If this is the case, then it would be a good idea to include the following events.

- Closing of the Iron Foundry
- The post-WWII tourist boom

Once you've chosen the historical events, it's time to write more narration. Start by copying and pasting your historical events list into the beginning of your editing script. Then go through the list and replace each historical event heading with a sentence of narration, just as you did with present-day issues. Try to make the history section come alive by writing exciting narration and including colorful events. Write an introductory paragraph of narration at the very beginning of the video, summarizing the character of the community and the basic topics it presents.

Before you're finished with the history section, you need to pick out the historical photos you'll want to use. Go back to your log and start copying and pasting the timecodes of each photo into your historical editing script. It's often best to have a number of photographs ready to use for each historical event because one narration sentence can last long enough to require three or more photographs on screen.

EXAMPLES OF NARRATION FROM THE SWANTON, VERMONT, COMMUNITY VIDEO

NARRATOR: Swanton Opening Paragraph

Swanton is a bustling agricultural and industrial community, located just south of the Canadian border in Franklin County, Vermont. Surrounded by farms, wetlands, the Missisquoi River, and Lake Champlain, Swanton has close ties to the land, as well as to its history as a cultural crossroads. With a changing economy, and with nearby Chittenden County growing at a dramatic rate, Swanton now faces some of its greatest challenges and opportunities ever.

NARRATOR: Swanton History

The first human settlers arrived in the Swanton area before 9000 B.C. As early as 6000 B.C., ancestors of the Native American Abenaki tribe began living at a site now known as "John's Bridge." For thousands of years, the ancient Abenakis inhabited the region, naming the river "Missisquoi"—a term meaning "Place of the Flint." Missisquoi was an important region in prehistory, a crossroads between trade routes to the south as far as the Caribbean, and as far north as the tip of Labrador. . . .

In 1963, to commemorate Swanton's charter from England, a pair of swans was given to the town as a gift from Queen Elizabeth II. Two swans, Sam and Betty, still reside on the village green today. . . .

In the first month of the 1970s, Swanton was hit by one of the worst disasters in its history: the Downtown Fire of 1970. The fire began in a store on Merchant's Row before midnight, and soon encompassed the entire historic block. Strong winds caused the inferno to spread across the street, destroying another block of buildings in the process. By the time the flames died down the following morning, Swanton's downtown district lay in smoldering ruins.

During the 1970s, Swanton struggled to rebound from the devastating fire, rebuilding its business district in a modern style.

NARRATOR: Establish Present Day Transition

Today Swanton remains a diverse, close-knit community that maintains strong ties to neighboring cities both north and south of the Canadian border. Nestled between rich farmland and an expansive wilderness area, Swanton has managed to retain a distinct rural character while facing new challenges for the twenty-first century.

NARRATOR: Establish Present Day Character—Canada

Swanton's proximity to Canada gives the town an international flair, with strong cultural and economic influences from Quebec.

NARRATOR: Abenaki

Swanton features three distinct cultural groups: "Anglo," French-Canadian, and Abenaki. The Abenakis, in particular, have had a strong influence on Swanton's character. Comprising 20 percent of the current population, the Abenakis have made Swanton their official tribal headquarters. In recent years the tribe has sought federal recognition, a struggle that has intensified after the discovery that parts of Swanton cover ancient Abenaki burial grounds. . . .

The final step for the history section is to include in your editing script any relevant interview clips. Any sound bites you have of residents telling tales about their town's history should be included. These interviews will really help to punch up the historical section and give it some variety.

Planning Themes for Montages

You're almost done with your editing script. The only task that remains is to plan out a few "montages" for the documentary. A montage is simply a series of shots that are generally set to music. A famous example of a montage would be the training sequence in "Rocky" when Stallone works out and then climbs the stairway. Another well-known montage is the space-docking sequence in "2001: A Space Odyssey" set to the tune of "The Blue Danube." Montages can be used to spice up a documentary, making it more appealing to an audience by illustrating concepts visually and artistically.

Montages should accompany any topics that lend themselves well to visual images. Montages could show:

- major landmarks in town;
- rush-hour traffic;
- a sequence of annual town events, or recreational or athletic activities; or
- paintings from art galleries.

Once you come up with ideas for four or five montages, go back to your log and look over the B-roll you have. Any shot that seems remotely related to the montage theme should be noted in your script. Just copy and paste together a list of potential shots, and insert this list between the topic sections. Montages can also be a great way to begin and end a video.

ARRANGING EDITING FACILITIES

As we mentioned at the beginning of this report, the editing phase of your Community Video requires you to get your hands on some sort of semi-professional editing system. Today's professional editors use nonlinear computer editing systems, such as *AVID, Media 100, Adobe Premiere*, or *Final Cut Pro*. Nonlinear editing is the process of transferring your footage to the hard drive of a computer where you can manipulate, edit, rearrange, and organize the images in just about any way you can imagine. When you're finished doing your digital magic, you can then send the final product back to videotape or even send it over the Internet. If you already have editing software installed on your own computer (and enough space on your hard drives), you're way ahead of the game. If not, regardless of your budget limitations, there is always a way to find an editing system.

There are many places in your community likely to have editing systems. These may include colleges and high schools, public access stations, video production companies, and private businesses. You probably can't afford to pay hourly commercial rates. Try to arrange an editing system for a block of time at a discount or, in the best case, for free. Remember that the video project is designed to benefit your community, and when people learn about your project, they may be willing to help. When you approach someone, arm yourself with fresh copies of newspaper articles or any other information you have generated for the project. Your editor may be able to help you find a system that works for your budget.

> *Nonlinear editing is the process of transferring your footage to the hard drive of a computer where you can manipulate, edit, rearrange, and organize the images in just about any way you can imagine.*

A quick and easy potential source for basic editing equipment is a local cable-access station. According to a federal law created in 1980, any region's cable TV system must provide for its community a station for ordinary citizens to produce and air their own programming. As long as you offer to broadcast the video on public access (which you will want to do anyway), these stations should be happy to let you use their systems. The only minor drawbacks of public access are that (1) editing systems are often only available a few hours at a time because they are so heavily booked for other shows, and (2) the editing systems available are not usually state-of-the-art. Despite that limitation, they will get the job done.

The other viable option these days is to set up a private nonlinear editing system. You'll need access to a computer that can handle video editing, with 300 or more Megahertz of processing speed, 200 or more Megabytes of RAM, video capture cards, and at least 20-30GB of SCSI hard drive space. You'll also need to spend about $500 for editing software such as *Adobe Premiere* or *Final Cut Pro*, unless you have access to it from another source. The new Macintosh G4 systems are a popular and cost-efficient choice, with 400-500 MHz, firewire inputs, lots of RAM, and 30GB of SCSI hard drive space already included.

EDITING YOUR COMMUNITY VIDEO
Editing typically takes place in a small room, with at most an editor, a producer, and a director overseeing the process. This process probably has more impact on the final outcome of a video, especially documentary projects, than any other single element. Editing can be very detailed, time consuming, and subjective. An important issue in editing a Community Video is how to involve the community in a process that is inherently so exclusive.

The answer: go back to the steering committee. Their biggest role in post-production will be to review a submitted editing script, check out draft versions of the video as it's being edited, and represent a balanced public consensus on various topics that may feature conflicting perspectives. This is not to say the committee will be sitting in the editing room looking over the poor editor's shoulder all day, but they will want to come in from time to time to provide input at various stages in the process. This is a good way to ensure that the final product has been checked for balance and accuracy. The committee can also provide input concerning the tone, pace, and style of the edited video to best reflect the community's character. Be certain to establish open lines of communication between the editing room and the steering committee during this stage so that everyone has a chance to help produce the final product; after all, it's a *Community Video*.

Music
Music can add more to the emotional impact of a Community Video than any other single element. Opening and closing sequences, montages, landscape shots, and historical narratives can all be immeasurably enhanced by the proper use of scoring. Whether you're using original compositions from your community or borrowing from store-bought CDs, it's vital to keep in mind that, just as the right music makes a huge positive difference, the wrong music will spoil even the best video project. Consult with your steering committee about music choices on an early version of your video to ensure that what you find appealing is just as appropriate for the group as a whole.

An important issue in editing a Community Video is how to involve the community in a process that is inherently so exclusive. The answer: go back to the steering committee.

For more information on video copyright . . .

Two excellent books on video copyrights, titles, music clearances, and release information are by Hollywood attorney Mark Litwak: *Dealmaking in the Film and Television Industry* and *Contracts for the Film and Television Industry*, published by Silman–James Press. Litwak also runs a good website: www.marklitwak.com.

Music Clearances and Rights

If you plan to screen your finished Community Video for the enjoyment of the public, you will definitely need to consider getting music clearances and rights for all copyrighted music you use in the project. This is something artists and publishers are absolute sticklers about. It's one thing to use copyrighted music on a video that stays in the historical society and is seen only by a few members now and then (like a wedding video); it's a completely different thing to use copyrighted music in a video that screens for several hundred people in a theater or on cable-access television. You will need to get permission for each copyrighted piece of music you use, even if it's only a few second's worth, and chances are that major recording artists and their publishers will be very difficult to get permission from without major financial expenditures. For this reason, consider using local or regional music that might be more affordable and is also in the spirit of the Community Video Project. For example, on the Swanton video we used only local Vermont-based music for which getting permission was an easy task, as the musicians were familiar with and sympathetic to the project. For the Fruita video, we used pre-licensed music that the regional PBS station owned all rights and clearances to for public broadcast purposes. Listen to the music on these videos, which are on the DVD included in this report. Taking care of music rights in the short run may save you a huge hassle down the road.

Credits and Titles

As you're preparing your final editing script, be absolutely certain to make a thorough list of all the names, titles, and information you plan to include in the video project. Have the steering committee review the following for accuracy:

- The on-screen name and personal description that will appear for each interviewee

- The credits listing all the people who made the actual video and their job titles

- The credits listing all the financial contributors

- The credits listing anyone and everyone, including businesses and organizations, who helped facilitate the making of the video

- The credits listing sources for all music, photos, and other added content

Being as thorough as possible with credits and titles will ensure that no one's feelings get hurt (or worse) due to a minor error in spelling or by an oversight on someone's part.

Once you have checked everything thoroughly, you're ready for the premiere.

PART 5

Premiering Your Video: Taking the Show on the Road

By now, word is out that a movie has been made about the community and that many familiar faces of local friends, neighbors, and relatives will be appearing in the finished product. Anticipation of the finished video should be building. Your job now is to harness this excitement and use it to bring the community together as a whole.

What's the best way to premiere your video? First, remember your goals. You definitely want the premiere to bring a large number of people together. You also want an opportunity for the audience to reflect on what they saw and heard in the video, and to think about ways they can use this information to visualize the future. Finally, you would like the audience to begin the process of creating their ideal vision for the community.

This is a lot to ask for one night. To get started, let's bring the community together for a fun-filled Grand Premiere to celebrate the completion of the video. In subsequent showings, you will want the community to use the video to begin the hard work of shaping the future of their community through strategic planning and other activities.

THE GRAND PREMIERE

The Grand Premiere is your chance to showcase your work to the community. The premiere screening will be ground zero for a video's long-term impact on a community. Viewers will form their first impressions of whether the video is moving, provocative, and timely. Viewers will also have opinions about how the video can be used to foster community dialogue and action.

You don't want people rushing for the door once the video is completed. Food will help people socialize before the screening and will keep them in the building while you discuss the video's implications.

Bringing your community together physically to celebrate the completion of a Community Video Project is an extremely important part of the process.

Things You Will Need

Here are things to consider when planning a premiere screening.

Find an appropriate venue. You want a space that can seat, say, 100 people, where you can serve food, and where the audience can socially interact at the completion of the video. The space should be sufficiently dark to watch the movie and free from outside noise. You will also want to be sure the space is ADA accessible. School gyms or auditoriums, the town hall, or a church social hall might be appropriate screening places. The video could even be screened outdoors in a public park after sunset, provided you have a contingency plan if the weather does not cooperate.

Pick an appropriate time. People have busy lives. That's one reason you produced the video in the first place. Try to pick a time when you think people in your community can best get together. In Swanton, Vermont, a Community Calendar was created reflecting every organization's meetings so that the screening would not conflict with other community activities. In our experience, evening screenings attract more people than those set during the day on Saturdays. The video could also be shown as part of another organization's event, such as a chamber of commerce annual meeting. However, make sure the video receives the attention it is due and that everyone in the community feels welcome to attend. Two other considerations. First, you might want a prominent public official to welcome people to the event, so make sure the screening fits with the public official's schedule. Second, you owe this all to your steering committee. Make sure you pick a time everyone on the committee can attend. The time you spend thanking everyone who helped you also helps the crowd build up its own buzz in anticipation of the video.

Supply food. People enjoy food. Check with a local restaurant, a school culinary class, or ask for volunteers to make sure there are plenty of refreshments. You don't want people rushing for the door once the video is completed. Food will help people socialize before the screening and will keep them in the building while you discuss the video's implications. If you plan far enough ahead, you can reward your caterer with a spot in the credits.

Have your equipment ready. There are some basic items you need to properly host a screening:

- A projector capable of showing your video
- A Video Cassette Recorder (VCR)
- A screen
- Lots of chairs

These days, most high school and college auditoriums already come equipped with most of these items, and if you are screening your video in this type of venue, you're all set. In many cases, however, you will need a portable video projector.

High-quality video projectors can be rented at very reasonable rates. Generally, a half-day rental can run as low as $200. A large business in your community may have a projector they use for Power Point projections. County agricultural extension offices also often have high-quality video projection equipment. As a last resort, you could borrow a large screen TV. These are not ideal for premiere showings, but could be appropriate in smaller, subsequent showings.

A projection screen should be easy to procure from a local school. Projecting the video onto a white wall, or hanging white sheets on the wall are other possibilities. A good VCR should be relatively easy to come by. If possible, use a "four-head" VCR for the highest quality output into the video projector. Be resourceful!

The sound system is the other major piece of equipment needed to host a quality public screening. The professional way to set up a sound system is to rent an amplifier, a sound mixing board, and two big public address speakers placed on either side of the screen. For this type of setup, it is advisable to find someone local who has had experience mixing live audio, either for a radio station or for a local band. This person should show up with equipment at least an hour before the crowd arrives to experiment with sound levels and to play sample clips from the actual video.

If you are unable to rent an amplifier, mixing board, and professional speakers, you can always use the do-it-yourself approach; a good home stereo will work fine as long as you have a good amplifier (or a good stereo receiver), a pair of decent-sized speakers, and lots of speaker wire. We recommend using speakers and an amplifier with ratings of 100 watts each or higher.

Setting up the Screening Equipment

If you're using a smaller, portable video projector, you'll find that it needs to sit no more than about 30 feet from the screen in order to project an image correctly. When you set your screen and chairs up in the room, be sure to make an aisle about four feet wide down the center of the room. This will leave room for a table or cart to hold the projector, VCR, and stereo receiver. We usually put the video projector on a small table, with our VCR and amplifier stacked underneath the table or behind the projector. Watch this island of equipment like a hawk to ensure that no one bumps into it or trips over it during a screening!

Wiring the system is easy. For optimal acoustic results, place a speaker on either side of your screen and run the speaker wires back along the sides of the room to your amplifier (be certain to tape the speaker wires to the floor to keep people from tripping on them). Your amplifier plugs into the "audio out" jacks of your VCR, and the video projector plugs into the

The professional way to set up a sound system is to rent an amplifier, a sound mixing board, and two big public address speakers placed on either side of the screen.

PART 5 HIGHLIGHTS:

Taking the show on the road . . .

- Pick an appropriate time and venue for the premiere. Make sure food is available.

- Equipment you will need includes:
   1. a projector capable of showing your video;
   2. a Video Cassette Recorder (VCR);
   3. an audio system with amplifier and speakers;
   4. a screen; and
   5. lots of chairs.

- To promote the event, issue press releases, invite people, spread word via e-mail chains, and be a guest on talk radio.

- Take a deep breath, give a brief introduction before the main event, thank everyone who has participated, and show the video.

- Conduct a feedback session immediately after the video to begin the process of leading the community to act on the vision established through the Community Video Project process.

- Other uses for the video include:
   1. kicking off strategic planning forums;
   2. enhancing the municipal planning process;
   3. use in schools or by other organizations, and
   4. broadcast on cable access television. (Public Broadcasting stations are likely to require "Beta"-quality video.)

- Evaluate your video. Ask yourself, "How do I know the Community Video made a difference?"

"video out" jack of your VCR. The VCR is the central playback device; audio goes out through the stereo system, video goes out through the projector. Simple!

Promoting the Event

Once you've got your screening venue and date locked down, it's time to spread the word about the screening. If you did a good job of promoting the video back in pre-production and production, much of your work is already done for you. However, keep in mind that many people in the community still have no knowledge of the video project. Getting these people to convene for a screening is the next goal. It's just a matter of letting them know something big and exciting is about to happen. Here's how to do it.

Invite people. Send invitations to everyone who was interviewed for the project, every crew member, everyone on the steering committee, every prominent member of the community for whom you have an address, and all your friends, relatives, and neighbors. Sending invitations out before publicly announcing the screening will make recipients feel like honored VIPs. Be sure to mention food.

E-mail. Encourage people involved in the video to e-mail their friends and colleagues.

Newspaper. Local newspapers tend to be the most effective channel through which to publicize a screening event. Readers see a date and time in print, clip the article, and post it on their refrigerators. Ideally, you've developed a good relationship with your local newspaper during pre-production and production. Write a press release that captures the excitement of the premiere. There's a good chance your local paper will run it verbatim. Follow the tips for press releases in Part 2 of this report.

Radio. Phone local radio stations and ask them to announce the screening date. Offer your availability to be on a live radio talk show or to give a news interview. If you do get on the air, just remember to relax and have fun, and mention the exact time and location of the screening several times.

Other opportunities. Use your judgment. Put notices on public bulletin boards. Make an announcement at other meetings, such as a Rotary Club, and ask if you can address their members about the Video Project.

THE SCREENING

As the big night approaches, you will probably get nervous. You want everything to go just as planned to ensure that your Community Video makes a lasting impression on all who see it. The hard work of producing and promoting is behind you; what remains is the screening. To help you get ready, we've put together another checklist to provide some guidelines as you prepare and oversee the screening event.

Food. Food will be the first thing your audience will notice when they walk in the room. Make sure people are comfortable and glad they came. You've got enough going on tonight, so make sure someone else has taken charge of food.

Setting up the room. Place projector and speakers in their appropriate places in the front of the room. Arrange the chairs with an aisle down the center. Make sure people in the back can see the screen, and that the food table is accessible but not in the way.

Test picture and sound. Set the equipment up and give it a test run. Be sure all your equipment will operate perfectly before you turn down the lights. Check that the picture is in focus and the sound is at the right level. Tape down the wires and secure the table. The videotape should be cued up a few seconds before the video begins. At the start of the program, all you should have to do is push "play." One important note: it looks very unprofessional to test actual clips of the video in front of the audience before the main show begins! Be certain that your system is working and cued up properly before anyone takes a seat. Keep the level of anticipation as high as possible!

Showtime

As people begin arriving, have one or two ushers stationed at the front entrance of the venue to guide people to their seats if necessary. Let the crowd mingle and chat for a few minutes. This will only increase anticipation of the video. Remember, no screening ever begins exactly on time.

When it's time to introduce the festivities, take a deep breath, go in front of the crowd, and begin by explaining the goals of the Community Video Project: that the purpose is to bring a community together to take a good look at itself. Thank everyone by name who assisted at any step, from steering committee members in pre-production to the public access station or schools that donated equipment during production to sponsors and crew members.

Explain during your introduction that there will be a feedback session after the screening, as well as a reception with refreshments. Have an order form prepared for people to order videos and have copies of the video for sale at the screening.

After your opening remarks, introduce the guest speaker or speaker of honor, if you have one. This person will make opening remarks and then introduce the much-awaited Community Video. Lower the lights and let it roll!

During a screening, it's often gratifying to watch the expressions on people's faces as they take in the presentation. Their attention will be glued to the screen as they see old photographs, familiar faces, and everyday locations that look larger than life on screen. Laughter might erupt from time to time as people interviewed in the video make animated or off-the-cuff comments. By the time the lights go up again, the audience's view of their own community ideally will have taken on new meaning.

THE FEEDBACK SESSION

With a variety of topics and ideas now fresh in people's minds, it's important to seize the moment and gauge the audience's immediate reactions to the video. A designated moderator should pose an array of thoughtful and discussion-provoking questions.

- What are people's initial reactions to the portrayal of the community?

- What do people feel about the video's emphasis or lack of emphasis on various topics?

- What does the video say about the town's sense of community as a whole and the direction in which it's headed? How could this message be more accurate?

- What does the video reveal to be the greatest strengths of the community as it now exists? Its weaknesses?

- What does it suggest are the greatest opportunities the community faces? Its greatest challenges?

- What have the community and its citizens already done to take advantage of opportunities and to respond to challenges? What can they do in the future?

With a variety of topics and ideas now fresh in people's minds, it's important to seize the moment and gauge the audience's immediate reactions to the video.

For more information about strategic planning . . .

There are many strategic planning resource guides available. The process in Morristown was guided by the Antioch New England Institute's *Engaging Citizens, Building Communities* program (ANEI@antiochne.edu). Reports that are especially designed for rural communities include:

- *Strategic Planning: Threats and Opportunities for Planners*, edited by John M. Bryson and Robert C. Einsweiler (Chicago: APA Planners Press, 1988);

- *Strategic Planning in Local Government*, edited by Roger Kemp (Chicago: APA Planners Press, 1992);

- *The Economic Renewal Guide: A Collaborative Process for Sustainable Community Development* by Michael Kinsley (Snowmass, Colo.: Rocky Mountain Institute, 1997); and

- *Take Charge: Economic Development in Small Communities* by the North Central Regional Center for Rural Development (for more information, consult www.exnet.iastate.edu/pages/communications/farm98/services/takecharge.html or Stuart Huntington at the Iowa State University in Ames, Iowa, 515-294-2973)

These types of questions should generate some lively discussion and may even encourage some heated responses. The point of this session is to begin to focus the energy of the crowd toward envisioning the future of the community. It can be very helpful to videotape this feedback session or appoint someone to take notes for future reference. Before the crowd disperses, it's worth the effort to pass a clipboard around the room with a sign-up sheet of names, street addresses, phone numbers, and e-mail addresses. This list of screening attendees can be particularly useful when trying to inspire and mobilize concerned citizens to work on a project or sit on a specific committee in the future.

OTHER USES FOR YOUR VIDEO
Using the Video as Part of a Strategic Planning Forum

Many communities use strategic planning forums to involve citizens in the creation of strategies and projects to improve community well being. The biggest challenges in organizing a strategic planning forum can be: (1) to get a large number of interested citizens to participate, and (2) to keep citizens excited about the process once they have agreed to give up their time to attend the strategic planning forum.

Showing the Community Video as a kick-off to a strategic planning forum is a great way to recruit people to attend and capture their attention. There is a good chance that a number of the citizens you would like to have at the strategic planning forum are also the people you interviewed to be in the video. Other citizens will come because they want to see their community on video, including friends, family, and neighbors.

The first step of a strategic planning model is to determine where the community is now in its evolution as a community. Usually a great deal of background data about the community is presented as a way for residents to reflect on their current circumstances. Data is essential to the process, but it takes a skilled presenter to make the data exciting. The Community Video is an alternative way of presenting background information on the community and starting the process of getting citizens to imagine how things can be in the future.

In Morristown, Vermont, the Community Video premiered between soccer games during homecoming weekend at a local school. Although the attendees discussed the video while they stood on the sidelines and watched the second soccer game, the premiere event did not provide a time for people to reflect on the implications of what was said in the video. However, the video was shown a second time the following month at a strategic planning event called "Morristown, Our Town."

Approximately 80 people attended the community forum, although the organizers acknowledge that perhaps 20 came only to see the video and didn't stay for the entire session. The organizers reported that the video hit the pulse of the community, raised awareness about issues, and gave folks a sense of pride and community. The people who came were excited to see people they knew. The video made them proud to be living in Morristown. They approached the rest of the strategic planning session with a confidence that they could make Morristown an even better place to live. By the end of the day, four working groups formed to:

- strengthen the downtown;

- develop a community arts center;

- preserve rural character; and

- build recreational trails.

THE MORRISTOWN, VERMONT, STRATEGIC PLANNING AGENDA

"Morristown—Our Town" Community Forum
November 6, 1999, 9:00 a.m.–4:00 p.m., Morrisville Elementary School

8:30	**REGISTRATION AND REFRESHMENTS**
9:00	**WELCOME AND INTRODUCTIONS** Goals for the day "Who's here?" An activity to break the ice.
9:15	**MORRISTOWN VIDEO** Introductory remarks by representative from The Orton Family Foundation and showing of Morristown video.
9:50	**PRESENTATIONS ON RECENT COMMUNITY AND ECONOMIC DEVELOPMENT EFFORTS** Updates on activities undertaken over the past decade related to community/economic development.
10:15	**WHERE SHOULD MORRISTOWN BE HEADED?** "What would you like to see Morrisville/Morristown look like and be like in 20 years?" (Small groups)
11:00	**BREAK**
11:15	**Creating a Collective Vision** Based upon the small group work, we will collectively develop a vision for Morristown. (Large group)
11:45	**ACHIEVING THE VISION: IDENTIFY POTENTIAL PRIORITY PROJECTS** Identify potential projects that can be implemented. (Small groups)
12:30	**LUNCH**
1:30	**SELECT PRIORITY PROJECTS** Review potential projects identified during small group sessions and select priority projects. (Large group)
2:30	**SETTING A COURSE OF ACTION** Based upon projects identified as priorities in previous session, define project goals, identify potential obstacles, determine action steps and proposed timeline, and set date for next meeting. (Small groups)
3:45	**WRAPPING UP** Small groups report back on projects. Summary of accomplishments for the day, review of next steps, and timeline.
4:00	**ADJOURN**

Source: Paul Markowitz, Antioch New England Institute

It is also important to note that because the video showed Morristown as a very family oriented and desirable place to live, Copley Hospital in Morristown ordered five copies of the video to send to doctors they were hoping to recruit to Morristown.

Enhancing the Municipal Planning Process

The Town of Brandon, Vermont, opened the public involvement process for rewriting the municipal plan by holding a visioning workshop. The Brandon Community Video was shown at the beginning of the workshop to encourage the 20 participants to think about the future. Approximately a third of the participants had already seen the video.

At the conclusion of the screening, a planner with the Rutland Regional Planning Commission led the group in a discussion of whether the video was an accurate portrayal of Brandon. There was discussion about the video's portrayal of truck traffic through the historic downtown as the major issue facing the community. (The Town Manager had already used the video to demonstrate to the area's Vermont legislative delegation the seriousness of the traffic issue.)

The truck discussion spurred the participants to think about other issues. Participants wrote out their own visions for how they would like to see Brandon in the future, and one participant wrote a letter to the newspaper about her vision. Each month the planning group meets to discuss a different section of the municipal plan, such as housing. Participants constantly refer back to portions of the video to compare it to their own future vision for Brandon.

School Use

Ideally, you've had someone from the local school on the steering committee, and students have been interviewed or served as interns, helping you cart your equipment around. Contact the social studies teachers at your local high school and offer the video for their use in history, civics, planning, economics, or film-making classes. Make yourself available to talk with students about the making of the video and its implications.

Organizations

Put a copy of your video in the hands of a wide variety of community groups. You should have a copy at the library, the historical society, and the chamber of commerce, with senior groups, or with any others who would make a good audience. For county fairs or other exhibits, you might want to purchase an "unending loop tape" that will continue to play the video without any rewinding.

Cable Access Television

As mentioned in the section about production, there is a federal law requiring every cable company nationwide to designate one channel as a "public access" station, which the cable company is required to run and finance. You may have already borrowed much of your equipment from a cable access station in return for promising to broadcast your video on the station.

Public access stations are generally thrilled to get their hands on well-edited, thoughtful, locally oriented programming. For a public access premiere, it's a good idea to contact a station manager or local talk show host and ask if you can broadcast your video as a feature of an existing show. If permission is granted, you might offer to be interviewed live before the video is shown and perhaps follow up afterwards with call-in questions from viewers. In a way, this is a nice complement to the live feedback session after a screening. Another advantage of airing the Community Video as part of an established show is that you already have some level of guaranteed viewership.

Public Broadcasting

PBS stations are becoming increasingly discriminating about their programming. There is a good chance they will demand video produced in high resolution to Beta-SP or Digital Beta quality, and, unfortunately, your digital camera only approximates Beta quality. You have to decide who the audience for the video will be. If you believe your video is of regional or statewide significance, or that people outside your region will clearly be interested in what your community has to say about itself, it won't hurt to seek access to a public broadcasting airing of your Community Video.

Keep in mind that PBS stations plan their broadcast schedules months in advance. Your best bet is to call up the station's programming director and explain the Community Video Project. Don't offer to send the actual tape initially; instead offer to fax the programming director additional information. Then immediately fax the programming director copies of a press release about the Community Video being readied for broadcast, and a copy of the most prominent article or review that the video has received. Be sure not to fax too much information; the point right now is just to whet the station's appetite. Follow up the next day with an offer to show the video itself. If the programming director is interested, immediately send a copy of the video along with any press materials you have.

In Fruita, Colorado, we were able to arrange a co-production with the regional PBS station, KRMJ, discussing in advance what the technical requirements of the video would be. It turned out that Beta SP would be necessary to air the finished video on broadcast television in that region. Also, the total running length had to be 26 minutes to accommodate public service announcements. Working with the station in advance helped us to create a project that both served the community of Fruita and fulfilled regional programming guidelines. The Fruita video is on the DVD enclosed in this report.

EVALUATING YOUR VIDEO

"Community" is a word people in America use all the time to describe where they live. Unfortunately, the meaning of this word is often abstract and describes nothing more than people living in close proximity to one another, without necessarily interacting. This does not mean that people don't *want* to interact. Often, they're insulated from one another by the circumstances of modern life in an individually oriented society. As you evaluate your Community Video Project, ask yourself what you expected to achieve. We hope your goal has been to engage more people in your community in the process of thinking about and taking action on the things they care about for the future. Use the excitement of creating a Community Video to encourage your community to convene, reflect, visualize, and act.

To evaluate your success, you must measure what your video has achieved. When you ask yourself the next set of questions, think about how you will know if these things have happened. Determine a set of indicators that will tell you the answer to the questions.

Has the community come together to make and view the video? Who was involved in planning? Who was interviewed? Who contributed archival material? Who donated money or in-kind resources? Who watched the video?

As you evaluate your Community Video Project, ask yourself what you expected to achieve. We hope your goal has been to engage more people in your community in the process of thinking about and taking action on the things they care about for the future.

Through the planning process, the people interviewed, and the number of times the video has been shown in the community, who has reflected on the circumstances of the past and the issues facing the future? In what planning or visioning activities have you seen people get involved? What are the issues they have uncovered?

What is the future that has been visualized by your community? What is the vision of the video? How does the video's vision compare with that of people who watch it?

What have people done to move toward their vision? What are the concrete actions that have taken place connected to the issues in the video?

A Community Video Project exploits the natural sense of excitement people feel when something outside their normal daily routine draws them together in public. It can capture people's attention in a world where attention is valuable and vigorously sought. It can inspire people to contribute ideas and visions to a common interest—their community. Furthermore, it can lead them to act on those ideas and visions. Best of all, a Community Video Project can help restore actual meaning to the word "community" and make people remember how good it feels to be part of a whole.

APPENDIX A. GLOSSARY

3/4-inch U-matic tapes   An older videotape stock format renowned for its durability. Largely replaced by Beta SP tapes as an industry standard, 3/4-inch tapes are still useful for analog edits where a durable tape stock is required to handle lots of rewinding, fast forwarding, and pauses.

analog   Traditional video which translates imagery into magnetic waves, as opposed to digital video which translates visual information into binary code. Similar in analogy to audio tape versus CDs.

backdrop   The background selected to appear in the camera's field of view, particularly behind interview subjects.

back light   One of three main lights in a lighting setup for interviews, usually placed to the rear left or right of an interview subject to create a three-dimensional lighting effect.

barn doors   Adjustable flaps on a halogen light that allow the width of its beam to be narrowed or widened.

Beta   A professional video format introduced by Sony long ago, which has become the industry standard for television and video production. Beta tapes are used with BetaCam cameras, providing video images with much higher resolution and durability than those produced by VHS or even Mini-DV formats. Beta tapes are available in 30- and 60-minute lengths from various manufacturers and are fairly expensive. BetaCams are extremely expensive and are usually rented, not purchased, by nonprofessional users. A newer digital version of Beta, called "DigiBeta," is a more recent industry standard for broadcast-quality video production.

broadcast quality   The quality of a video image, based on the tape stock and camera type used in its recording, necessary to meet requirement guidelines for television broadcast. Usually Beta tape and cameras or better are required to provide a high enough image quality for TV broadcast. Exceptions include reality-based TV shows and news clips shot by lay people.

B-roll   Secondary footage shot to augment or complement primary interview footage, usually comprised of locations shots, photos, and other material to use in cutaways.

chip   Specifically, the chip found in a video camera. Technically know as "charge-coupled devices" or "CCDs," the chips in a video camera process light waves into three separate colors (red, green, and blue) and translate them into magnetic impulses, which are then recorded on tape. A good video camera will have three separate chips that each process a separate color, creating a richer, more detailed image on tape. Less expensive cameras have one chip only.

copyright   Specifically referring to music, photos, or moving images that are privately produced material from a protected source. Be certain to get permission from the copyright holder (e.g., the record company, museum, or book publisher) to use any copyrighted music or imagery in your video.

credits   A list of every person and organization involved in the production of a video, usually appearing at the video's end. It is important to be thorough with credits as they are often the only way a video's participants are thanked publicly; omitting volunteer participants from the credits in a Community Video is politically unwise.

critical focus   A technique for focusing a video camera properly on a subject so that the subject remains in constant focus no matter how far in or out the camera zooms.

Digi-Beta   A new digital form of the venerable Beta video format (see Beta). A high quality, expensive new standard in video production and television broadcast, second only to High Definition.

digital   In the case of video production, "digital" implies that a camera translates visual information into binary code as a series of ones and zeros, as opposed to traditional video, which translates imagery into magnetic waves. Similar in analogy to audio tape versus CDs.

director   The person responsible for the look and feel of a video production, and often the person who will oversee how interviews are conducted and how the video is edited.

DV camcorder   A "digital video" camcorder, first introduced to the consumer market in 1995, that processes visual imagery as a digital binary signal, thus creating a high-quality image that is impervious to physical degeneration.

editing script   A flowchart of quotes, narration, and cutaway shots that is organized prior to editing a video, in order to make the editing process as quick and efficient as possible.

editor   The person responsible for editing a video. This person will usually run the editing system/editing software as well as make key decisions about how a video will be pieced together. Editing involves a good deal of creative decision making and is most often not done well by committee. A good editor is an absolute must.

fill light   Another of the three lights in a typical interview setup. A fill light is used to prevent shadows on a subject by "filling in" where the key and back lights don't overlap.

firewire cables   Special cables used to transmit binary information from digital cameras into a computer. Firewire allows for the greatest level of quality output from a digital camera.

fluorite lens   A special composite glass lens used by Canon on their better video cameras.

footage   Anything you shoot on tape with a video camera (e.g., "the footage I shot of that cougar eating a tourist at Mount Rushmore last May").

four-head VCR   A Video Cassette Recorder (VCR) with four recording and playback heads, which allows for a high-quality image and also allows the VCR to pause on a frame with no distortion.

framing the shot   Adjusting a camera on a subject so that the subject fills the camera's viewfinder and "frame" in a desired manner. A subtle and often artful process.

halogen bulbs   Light bulbs that shine at a much higher temperature than normal bulbs, producing a brighter, whiter light that more closely mimics the look of natural light. The preferred choice of lighting for any video production.

Hi-8   A video format introduced in the 1980s that offers higher-quality images than standard VHS, all on a little eight-millimeter tape that allowed for much smaller camera sizes.

interview clips   Individual snippets of video interviews that can be subsequently arranged together to create consistent topics and themes in a video.

JPEG file   A type of digital file typically used to compress and send photographs on computers. Other common types of computer photo files include TIF and GIF files.

key light   The third of three lights in a typical interview setup. The key light is the main light used for direct illumination, usually placed to the front left or right of a subject.

lavolier microphone   A small microphone used for interviews that can be inconspicuously placed on a subject without showing up on camera. Lavoliers can come with cables that attach to a camera or in a wireless version to be used with a small radio transmitter worn by a subject.

LCD screen   A Liquid Crystal Display, typically found on laptop computers, digital watches, and other small electronic appliances. Some video cameras have LCD screens that flip out to allow the user to see what the camera sees without having to peer through a viewfinder.

linear editing system   Also know as an analog editing system. An old system of editing that involves laying pieces of video material together in a linear fashion, working from the beginning of a time line towards its end. Typically, this system involves recording different bits and parts of source material onto one Master Tape, requiring the editor to piece a final video together without the luxury of shifting parts around to see how they fit in different organizational combinations. Largely replaced by *nonlinear editing*, which involves loading all source material into a computer and piecing it together any way you can think of, regardless of fixed order or time line.

logging footage   The process of watching all footage recorded for a video project and typing it line by line into a computer, in order to document what you have on tape for later use in editing. Tedious, but necessary; logging is the video equivalent of court stenography.

magic hour   The time of day when the sun is low in the sky (sunrise or sunset), creating a picturesque glow over the landscape or subjects you want to videotape. Short-lived but definitely preferable to outdoor shots at high noon, when sunlight is flat and harsh.

miking the shot   Placing a microphone on a subject or in a scene in order to assess sound levels before you begin shooting tape.

mini-DV tapes   The small digital tapes used in digital camcorders, usually priced under $20.

montage   A sequence of shots that creates an evocative or arousing visual array, best combined with stirring music, narration, or audio clips of interview quotes.

music clearances and rights (See *copyright*)

narrator   The person who tells a story. Typically a role best filled by someone with a good voice who can read eloquently and smoothly.

nonlinear editing system (see also ***linear editing system***)   An editing system in which video footage is loaded into a computer and then arranged using special editing software. This style of editing has countless advantages over its predecessor, linear editing, because it allows video footage to be combined in any number of ways without restriction. Today's nonlinear systems are increasingly affordable and easy to use, allowing lay people to become editors.

out takes   Pieces of video footage that aren't used in a final video production.

pan   The act of sweeping a camera from side to side, usually on a tripod.

playback deck   A machine specifically designated to play video tapes into an editing system, which eliminates the need to use the camera itself to play tapes.

post-production   The process that takes place after a video is shot, which involves editing all of the amassed footage together into a final product.

pre-production   The process that takes place before a video is produced, which includes arranging resources and staff, lining up interviews and locations, raising money, etc.

present-day narration   Narration that pertains to modern day topics, issues, and events.

producer   The person in charge of an entire video production, including the business and organizational aspects of making a video. This person may also serve as the director and sometimes even an editor of a video production.

production budget   The pre-allocated and itemized budget assembled before the start of a video production. Usually the responsibility of the producer.

production crew   The people who work on the actual production of a video, helping with everything from organizational tasks, to moving equipment, to running errands.

professional headphones   Headphones that are suitable for professional use, typically a bit more expensive than consumer or walkman headphones.

public access station A television station set up for the exclusive purpose of creating and broadcasting community-based programming. A good place to start when looking to produce a community video.

rack focus A type of camera focusing technique in which the lens is focused from a far away object in the background to a nearby object in the foreground, or vice versa. Used for dramatic effect.

RCA cables The basic cables that come with every modern television, stereo, and video camera, usually color-coded for ease of use.

reflector board A white or shiny board used to strategically reflect light for a shot.

release form A form that, when signed by an interview subject, grants a video producer the legal right to use the subject's interview and image in a video production.

resolution Term describing the visual quality of a video camera or video tape, often pertaining to the "lines of resolution" that measure the level of detail that a camera is able to capture in an image. Usually, the higher the resolution, the more crisp and detailed the image.

screening The act of showing a finished video to an audience.

shotgun microphone A long microphone, often mounted on a video camera, that picks up sounds from a specific direction, rather than from a variety of directions.

SMTPE timecode Term used to describe a system that assigns each frame of video footage a numeric code based on the 24-hour clock. A frame of SMTPE timecode might read 1:41:25, meaning a video frame found 1 hour, 41 minutes, and 25 seconds into a tape. Timecode is used to keep accurate track of where images and segments can be found on a given tape.

S-VHS "Super VHS" is a format designed years ago to create a high-quality image on a tape the same size as a standard VHS tape. Higher in quality but still relatively affordable, SVHS has largely been supplanted in use by Mini-DV. Note that an S-VHS player will play normal VHS tapes, but a VHS player will not play S-VHS tapes.

S-video cables Cables that break a video image into separate channels, allowing for higher quality image transfers from one source to another. Better than RCA, although digital cameras are best used with firewire cables if they are available and compatible with your system.

swish pans A rapid camera movement from side to side, used for action shots or dramatic effect.

three-point lighting A system used to light interviews whereby a subject is placed in the middle of three lights, enabling optimal use of light while preventing shadows or glare.

timecode (See also *SMPTE timecode*) Numeric code assigned to video footage so that it can be counted frame by frame. Usually a 4-digit code on a VCR or playback deck.

titles Words that appear over video footage, typically at the beginning to tell the viewer what the piece consists of, and during interviews to tell the viewer who is speaking.

tripod A three-legged adjustable stand used to hold a video camera.

VU meter A meter on a camera or sound recording deck that indicates the level of sound, in decibels.

white balance An important function on video cameras that tunes the camera in to a neutral shade of white, allowing all colors to appear in proper contrast. Usually an automatic function on nonprofessional video cameras. Especially important to pay attention to when moving from indoors to outdoors with a camera or vice versa.

zoom in/out The act of using a camera's telescopic lens to move a shot closer in to (or further away from) a subject. Can be used for dramatic effect. Overused by amateurs constantly.

APPENDIX B: USEFUL RESOURCES

Ascher, Steven, et al. 1999. *The Filmmaker's Handbook: A Comprehensive Guide for the Digital Age.* New York: Plume.

Baert, Luc, and Guido Vergolt. 1995. *Digital Audio and Compact Disc Technology.* Woburn, Mass.: Focal Press.

Beal, Steven. 2000. *The Complete Idiot's Guide to Making Home Videos.* Carmel, Ind.: Alpha Books.

Borwick, John. 1994. *Sound Recording Practice.* New York: Oxford University Press.

Brown, Steven E. 1998. *Nonlinear Editing Basics: Electronic Film and Video Editing.* Woburn, Mass.: Focal Press.

Desposito, Joseph, and Kevin Garabedian. 1998. *Complete Camcorder Troubleshooting and Repair.* Indianapolis, Ind.: Howard W. Sams & Co.

Hoffer, Avi. 1999. *Digital Guerilla Video: A Grassroots Guide to the Revolution.* Manhasset, N.Y.: CMP Books.

Jones, Frederick. 1998. *Desktop Digital Video Production.* New York: McGraw-Hill.

Litwak, Mark. 1994a. *Dealmaking in the Film and Television Industry.* Beverly Hills, Calif.: Silman-James Press.

_____. 1994b. *Contracts for the Film and Television Industry.* Beverly Hills, Calif.: Silman-James Press.

Malkiewicz, Kris. 1992. *Film Lighting.* New York: Simon and Schuster.

Musburger, Robert B. 1999. *Single-Camera Video Production.* Woburn, Mass.: Focal Press.

Oldham, Gabriella. 1992. *First Cut: Conversations with Film Editors.* Berkeley: University of California Press.

Pohlmann, Ken C. 1995. *Principles of Digital Audio.* New York: McGraw-Hill.

Rabiger, Michael. 1998. *Directing the Documentary.* Woburn, Mass. Focal Press.

Robinson, Andy. 1996. *Grassroots Grants.* Berkeley, Calif.: Chardon Press.

Roth, Cliff. 1997. *The Low Budget Video Bible.* Desktop Video Systems.

Sherman, Sharon R. 1998. *Documenting Ourselves: Film, Video, and Culture.* Lexington: University Press of Kentucky.

Soifer, Rosanne. 1997. *Music in Video Production.* Woburn, Mass.: Focal Press.

Videomaker Magazine. 1996. *The Videomaker's Handbook.* Woburn, Mass.: Focal Press.

Watkinson, John. 1994. *The Art of Digital Recording.* Woburn, Mass.: Focal Press.

Wiese, Michael. 1993. *Producer to Producer.* Studio City, Calif.: Michael Wiese Productions.

MAGAZINES

"Camcorder & Computer Video" (805) 644-3824

"DV Magazine" http://www.dv.com (415) 905-2200

"Moviemaker Magazine" http://www.moviemaker.com

"New Media Magazine" http://www.newmedia.com (650) 573-5170

"Sound and Vision Magazine" http://www.soundandvisionmag.com (212) 767-6000

"Videomaker" Magazine http://www.videomaker.com (530) 891-8410

"Videography Magazine" http://www.videography.com (212) 378-0400

WEB SITES

Cyber Film School (www.cyberfilmschool.com)

DigiEffects (Cinelook Software) (www.digiteffects.com)

Digital Cinema (www.tech-head.com)

Digital Idiots (www.digitalidiots.com)

DV Central (www.dvcentral.com)

Digital Video Editing (www.digitalvideoediting.com)

The DV Filmmaker's Report (e-mail newsletter) (www.dvfilmmaker.com)

Macintosh DV Resources (www.postforum.pair.com)

Mark Litwak (information on copyright) (www.marklitwak.com)

Nonlinear Editing Guide (www.nonlinear3.com)

Nationwide Public Access Stations (www.openchannel.se/cat/links2.htm)

Video Production Companies Directory (www.broadcastvideo.com/freelance)

RES: The Magazine of Digital Filmmaking (www.resmag.com)

CAMCORDER MANUFACTURERS

Sony DV Camcorders (800) 222-7669
(www.sel.sony.com/SEL/consumer/ss5/digitalvideo)

Canon Camcorders (800) OK-CANON

Canon Digital Camcorders (www.canondv.com)

Canon Hi-8 Camcorders (www.usa.canon.com/camcambin/camcorders/8mm)

JVC Camcorders (800) 882-2345 or (800) 252-5722
(www.JVC.com/cat_portable.jsp?index=0&productId=PRD1200001)

Panasonic Camcorders (800) 211-7262
(www.panasonic.com/consumer_electronics/video/index.htm)

MAIL-ORDER TRIPOD MANUFACTURERS

Benbo
(716) 328-7800
(www.saundersphoto.com)

Bogen Photo Corporation
(201) 818-9500
(www.bogenphoto.com)

Cartoni USA
(888) 227-8664 or (805) 520-6086
(www.cartoni.com)

Linhof
(800) 735-4373
(www.linhof.net)

Matthews Studio Equipment
(818) 843-6715
(www.matthewsgrip.com)

Sachtler Corporation of America
(516) 867-4900
(www.sachtler.com)

Velbon Tripod Company
(800) 423-1623
(www.velbon.com)

Vinten
(914) 268-0100
(www.vinten.com)

LIGHTING EQUIPMENT MANUFACTURERS

ERS

Arriflex
(914) 353-1400
(www.arri.com)

Beseler
(908) 862-7999
(www.beseler-photo.com)

Cine 60
(212) 586-8782

Hahnel USA
(715) 273-7799
(hahnel-usa.com/index.html)

Jasco Products
(800) 654-8483
(www.jascoproducts.com)

Lowel-Light Manufacturing
(800) 334-3426
(www.lowel.com)

NRG Research
(800) 753-0357
(www.nrgresearch.com)

Photoflex
(800) 486-2674
(www.photoflex.com)

Vanguard USA
(800)875-3322
(www.vanguardusa.com)

MICROPHONE MANUFACTURERS

Audio-Technica USA
(330) 686-2600
(www.audio-technica.com)

Azden Corporation
(516) 328-7500
(www.azdencorp.com)

Beyerdynamic Sales USA
(516) 293-3200
(www.beyerdynamic.com)

Nady Systems
(510) 652-2411
(www.nadywireless.com)

Samson Technologies
(516) 364-2244
(www.samsontech.com)

Sennheiser Electronic Corporation
(860) 434-9190
(www.sennheiserusa.com)

Shure Brothers
(847) 866-2200
(www.shure.com)

Telex Communications
(612) 884-4051
(www.telex.com)

CAMCORDER BATTERY MANUFACTURERS

Aardvark Batteries
(888) 883-4937
(www.aardvardbat.com)

Atbatt.com
(877) 4AT-BATT
(www.atbatt.com)

The Battery Bank
(800) 229-9449
(www.batterybank.com)

Batteries Direct
(888) 320-1212
(www.batteriesdirect.com)

E-Battery
(877) BATT2GO
(e-battery.com)

Go Battery
(888) GO-BATTERY
(www.gobattery.com)

MJM Electronic
(888) 226-4606
(www.mjmelectronic.com)

VIDEO GEAR COMPANIES

Adorama
(800) 223-2500
adorama@aol.com (e-mail)

Armato's
(800) 628-6801
(www.armatos.com)

B & H Photo/Video/Pro Audio
(800) 947-9925
(wwwbhphotovideo.com)

Beach Camera
(800) 634-1811
(www.beachcamera.com)

Camera Sound
(800) 477-0022
(www.camerasound.com)

Camera World
(800) 729-8933
(www.cameraworld.com)

DV Direct
(888) 383-8366
(www.dvdirect.com)

Elite Video
(800) 468-1996
(www.elitevideo.com)

Industrial Video Technology (rentals only)
(800) 362-7368
(www.rentgear.com)

Video Equipment.com (new/used equipment for sale)
(888)354-2510
(www.videoequipment.com/index3.htm)

Worldwide Video Enterprises
(800) 617-4686
(www.buydig.com)

MUSIC CLEARANCE RIGHTS
Mark Litwak, Attorney
(www.marklitwak.com/music_mpsound.htm)

NATIONAL DIRECTORY OF PUBLIC ACCESS STATIONS
(www.openchannel.se/cat/links2.htm)

NATIONAL VIDEO EQUIPMENT RENTAL COMPANY
Industrial Video Technology
(800) 362-7368
(www.rentgear.com)

NEW AND USED VIDEO EQUIPMENT FOR SALE
Videoequipment.com
(www.videoequipment.com/index3.htm)
(888) 354-2510

NATIONAL GUIDE TO VIDEO PRODUCTION COMPANIES
Broadcastvideo.com
(www.broadcastvideo.com/freelance)

VIDEO PRODUCTION MANUAL ON LINE
Digitalidiots.com
(www.digitalidiots.com)

STAFF:
CHECK DVD IN POCKET

C09434290

RENEWALS 458-2440

DATE DUE

DEC 1 1			

GAYLORD — PRINTED IN U.S.A.

UTSADT
Folio
PN
1992.94
.078
2001

JLM